MARTIN HEIDEGGER

A FIRST INTRODUCTION TO HIS PHILOSOPHY

MARTIN HEIDEGGER

A FIRST INTRODUCTION TO HIS PHILOSOPHY

BY

JOSEPH J. KOCKELMANS, PH.D.

1965

DUQUESNE UNIVERSITY PRESS

Pittsburgh, Pa.

EDITIONS E. NAUWELAERTS, LOUVAIN

GATEWAY TO REALITY

Engelbert J. van Croonenburg

Second edition. $3.25

PHENOMENOLOGY AND PHYSICAL
SCIENCE

Joseph Kockelmans

Spring 1966

CONTEMPORARY EUROPEAN THOUGHT
AND CHRISTIAN FAITH

Albert Dondeyne

Second edition. $5.75

ENCOUNTER

Remy C. Kwant

Second edition. $3.25

EXISTENTIAL PHENOMENOLOGY

William A. Luijpen

Fourth impression. $6.25

Library of Congress Catalog Card Number 64-8313
© 1965, by Duquesne University
Printed in the U. S. A. by
The Ad Press, Ltd., N. Y.

PREFACE

As the title of this small book indicates, it merely wants to provide a first elementary introduction to the philosophical thought of Martin Heidegger. It would be wrong therefore to seek here any new interpretation of this German philosopher or even a complete presentation of all his philosophical ideas. Still less should the specialists in contemporary philosophy expect to find here new perspectives. The only aim of this Introduction is to make it easier for the uninitiated to find a first access to Heidegger's ideas.

The Introduction is centered around a few of his major themes, mostly taken from *Being and Time*. Heidegger's other works are touched only to the extent that they throw light on the development of his thinking with respect to those themes.

The interpretation of Heidegger presented here has been largely guided by the studies of Alphonse de Waelhens, Albert Dondeyne, Walter Biemel, Ludwig Landgrebe, Bernard Welte, Bernard Löwith, and Bernard Delfgaauw. These studies are only occasionally referred to in the text, but for the benefit of the interested student we have listed them in the bibliography.

JOSEPH J. KOCKELMANS

The first translation of this work was made by Mrs. Therese Schrynemakers, partly revised by Dr. Arthur S. Schrynemakers, and submitted to a careful checking and rewriting by the undersigned. The latter has also added most of the divisions and subtitles throughout the work.

Preface

It has been read and approved by the author, who has added also the concluding chapter to this edition.

Anyone who is familiar with Heidegger's language knows how difficult it is to translate his work. Existing translations and studies of his books vary widely in their rendition of his technical terms. For this reason a choice had to be made to maintain uniformity and, in some cases, even another translation added to the growing list of variations.

DUQUESNE UNIVERSITY   HENRY J. KOREN, C.S.Sp.

TABLE OF CONTENTS

CHAPTER ONE

INTRODUCTION

Although Martin Heidegger is one of the most famous philosophers of our time and enjoys a world-wide reputation, little is known of his private life and personality. He himself is rather reticent on personal matters and his devoted friends and pupils have reverently respected his silence. The rare data on his life and personality mentioned in the extensive studies about Heidegger are not always reliable and often even conflicting with regard to important matters.

This reticence can perhaps, in part, be accounted for by his attitude toward the Nazi movement from 1933 until 1945. But, in view of the fact that Heidegger was already very uncommunicative about his private life long before 1933, other factors seem to play an important role as well.

When in 1914, on the occasion of receiving his doctorate at the age of twenty-four, he was required to submit an extensive autobiography, Heidegger confined himself to the following statement:

I, Martin Heidegger, was born on September 26, 1889, at Messkirch (Baden) as the son of Friedrich Heidegger, sexton and cellarer, and his wife Johanna, maiden name Kempf, both of the Catholic religion. After having attended the public school of my home town, I studied at the Gymnasium of Constance from 1903 until 1906, and after the third year I transferred to the Bertholds-Gymnasium in Freiburg-im-Breisgau, where I received my diploma in 1909. Until my oral examination for the doctorate I attended the university of Freiburg-im-Breisgau. During the first two years I attended lectures in philosophy and theology, after

1

1911 I concentrated mostly on philosophy, mathematics and the natural sciences, and during the last semester I added history.[1]

Whatever reasons he may have, Heidegger undoubtedly prefers to reveal as little as possible about himself. Sometimes this attitude has been linked to his opinion that, in order to understand someone's works, one needs to know little or nothing about the author's life. One day, while speaking about Aristotle, he dealt with that philosopher's life and personality in one sentence: "He was born, he worked and he died." When writing or lecturing on other philosophers, he never mentioned more about their private lives than he deemed necessary for an adequate understanding of their philosophy; in most cases this was next to nothing.

And yet, all this does not fully explain Heidegger's self-reticence. Nevertheless, we will not press for any deeper motives since we too want to respect Heidegger's wish. We will only mention some of the pertinent facts of his life.

Early Life and First Writings

As stated above, Heidegger was born in 1889 at Messkirch in Baden, as the elder of the two sons of Friedrich Heidegger. His only brother, of whom he is very fond, still resides in Messkirch.

After having attended the village school, he went to Constance. The most probable reason for attending the Gymnasium in that town was Heidegger's intention to study for the priesthood. Here for the first time he became acquainted with philosophy, which soon would become his main interest. Later he moved to Freiburg, where he completed his studies at the Gymnasium in 1909.

At the university of Freiburg, Heidegger at first studied theology and philosophy. After he had abandoned the idea of becoming a priest, he applied himself for some time

---

[1] *Die Lehre vom Urteil im Psychologismus,* Leipzig, 1914.

to mathematics and physics, but finally decided to devote his life to philosophy. During these years he spent much time reading the works of Franz Brentano.

As early as 1912, while still a student of philosophy, he published a short article on epistemology, entitled "The Problem of Reality in Modern Philosophy."[2] In this article Heidegger did not yet express a personal viewpoint but confined himself to defending the realism of Geyser, Messer and Kulpe against a psychologism that rejected all metaphysics. At this time there was no trace as yet of any influence exercised by Dilthey, Kierkegaard or Nietzsche.

In his doctoral dissertation, *The Theory of Judgment in Psychologism,*[3] he abandoned the traditional standpoint and took leave of Brentano's philosophy without, however, having arrived at genuinely personal insights.

Because of his frail health, Heidegger was exempted from military service until 1917; thus he was able to continue his studies at Freiburg during World War I. As early as 1916 he published his second book, *Duns Scotus' Doctrine of Categories and Meanings.*[4] The main basis of his study was the so-called *Grammatica speculativa,* but, as Grabmann has shown in 1926, this work was written by Thomas of Ehrfurt. Heidegger's study was a *Habilitationsschrift,* a probationary thesis, which entitled him to teach philosophy in Freiburg as *Privatdozent.*

Contacts and Influences

Although Heidegger composed his doctoral dissertation under the mentorship of A. Schneider, the influence of H. Rickert was already quite noticeable. Under the latter's guidance he wrote his "probationary thesis." However,

---

[2]"Das Realitätsproblem in der modernen Philosophie," *Philosophisches Jahrbuch der Görres-Gesellschaft,* vol. XXV (1912), pp. 353-363.

[3]*Die Lehre vom Urteil im Psychologismus.*

[4]*Die Kategorien- und Bedeutungslehre des Duns Scotus,* Tübingen, 1916.

in 1916 Husserl went to Freiburg, and the influence which he exerted on Heidegger there overshadowed that of Rickert. In 1920 Heidegger became Husserl's assistant and both thinkers worked in close cooperation until 1923.

In that year Nicolai Hartmann was instrumental in bringing Heidegger to Marburg with the rank of *professor ordinarius*. His friendship with Husserl continued, but in his thinking Heidegger gradually grew away from him. In Marburg, Heidegger befriended Rudolf Bultmann and thus came in contact with the theology of Karl Barth. Bultmann and Barth led him to Kierkegaard and Luther, whose works were thoroughly studied by Heidegger. During this period he also liked to occupy himself with the writings of Pascal and Dostoevsky.

Although Hartmann's personality and viewpoint differed considerably from those of Heidegger, both men shared a common desire for a renovation of ontology, and for some time they maintained very cordial relations. After at first having been critical of Max Scheler, Heidegger learned to appreciate him. Finally, during those years, he also befriended Karl Jaspers.

A New Philosophy

It was at Marburg that Heidegger composed, partly in connection with his university lectures, his main work *Being and Time*,[5] the first volume of which was published in 1927. In spite of the fact that this book presented great linguistic difficulties and intended to bring an entirely new way of philosophizing, it was widely read and enthusiastically approved by many of its readers. Heidegger became famous overnight and soon he was acclaimed as one of Germany's greatest philosophers.

In 1928 he returned to Freiburg as *professor ordinarius*. Husserl was then on the verge of retiring and, although it had become evident to him that Heidegger had deviated

---

[5]"Sein und Zeit. Erste Hälfte," *Jahrbuch für Philosophie und phänomenologische Forschung,* vol. VIII (1927), pp. 1-438.

from his own standpoint in many essential respects, he requested that Heidegger be made his successor. To the memorial volume offered to Husserl by his best known former students in 1929, on the occasion of his retirement, Heidegger contributed his remarkable essay *On the Essence of Ground*.[6]

In 1929 he also published an original historical study on Kant, explaining his own position with regard to Kant's philosophy, *Kant and the Problem of Metaphysics*.[7] And his inaugural address of July 24, 1929, was printed under the title *What is Metaphysics?*[8] This work is of great importance for an adequate understanding of *Being and Time*.

The Nazi Period

In 1933, the year in which Hitler came to power in Germany, Heidegger was appointed *Rector magnificus* of the university of Freiburg. In his inaugural address of May 27, 1933, entitled *The Self-Preservation of the German University*,[9] Heidegger openly favored the National-Socialistic Movement. After having heard his speech, one of his pupils remarked:

> In comparison to the numerous . . . speeches which professors of equal rank have given since the take-over of power, this philosophical and forceful speech is a little masterpiece. Service in the labor forces and in the armed forces merges with service in the realm of learning in such a way that, at the end of this speech, one no longer knows whether to study Diel's *Presocratics* or to march in the ranks of the Storm Troopers.[10]

---

[6]"Vom Wessen des Grundes," *Festschrift Edmund Husserl zum 70. Geburtstag gewidmet*, Ergänzungsband zum *Jahrbuch für Philosophie und phänomenologische Forschung*, Halle, 1929, pp. 71-100.
[7]*Kant und das Problem der Metaphysik*, Bonn, 1929.
[8]*Was ist Metaphysik?*, Bonn, 1929.
[9]*Die Selbstbehauptung der deutschen Universität*, Breslau, 1933.
[10]P. Hühnerfeld, *In Sachen Heideggers. Versuch über ein deutsches Genie*, Hamburg, 1959, pp. 57-58.

This speech undoubtedly was a great disappointment to many colleagues, friends and pupils. Heidegger has especially been blamed for abandoning his old friends, and foremost his master Husserl. Even the dedication to Husserl was omitted for some time after 1933 from the editions of *Being and Time,* although Heidegger was not personally to blame for this omission.

During the thirties, however, Heidegger gradually drew away from Hitler's regime, and in the following decade there was even an order forbidding him to publish. Throughout this dark period he wrote little. In 1937 he issued a treatise, *Hölderlin and the Essence of Poetry,*[11] in which he explained the fundamental principles of his philosophical aesthetics. In addition to a few more publications on *Hölderlin,*[12] in 1942 and 1943 he authored the well known booklets *Plato's Doctrine of Truth*[13] and *On the Essence of Truth,*[14] both of great importance for a good grasp of the development of Heidegger's thinking. To a 1947 reprint of the former, he added his well-known *Letter on Humanism.*[15]

Post-War Publications

When World War II ended, Heidegger withdrew— partly forced by circumstances and partly out of preference —into his ski hut at Todtnau near Freiburg. Until 1957, however, he continued with regular frequency to present lectures and addresses. And since 1950 he has published several works containing, for the most part, lectures which he delivered at Freiburg between 1928 and 1957. The

---

[11]"Hölderlin und das Wesen der Dichtung," *Das innere Reich,* München, 1936/37, pp. 1065-1078.

[12]*Hölderlins Hymne "Wie wenn am Feiertage,"* Halle, 1941. "Andenken," *Hölderlin. Gedenkschrift zu seinem 100. Todestag,* Tübingen, 1943, pp. 267-324. *Erläuterungen zu Hölderlins Dichtung,* Frankfurt a.M., 1944.

[13]"Platons Lehre von der Wahrheit," *Geistige Überlieferung,* vol. II (1942), pp. 96-124.

[14]*Vom Wesen der Wahrheit,* Frankfurt a.M., 1943.

[15]*Platons Lehre von der Wahrheit. Mit einem Brief über den "Humanismus,"* Bern, 1947.

following works deserve special mentioning: *Forest Trails* (1950),[16] *An Introduction to Metaphysics* (1953),[17] *Lectures and Essays* (1954),[18] *What Does Thinking Mean?* (1954),[19] *On the Question of Being* (1955),[20] *What is Philosophy?* (1956),[21] *The Thesis of Ground* (1957),[22] *Identity and Difference* (1957),[23] *On the Road Toward Language.*[24] His most recent publications are a two volume work on *Nietzsche*[25] and a commentary on the first book of Aristotle's *Physics: On the Essence and the Notion of Physics.*[26]

"Heimat"[27] *in the Black Forest*

Heidegger received the honorable invitation to come to Berlin and lecture with the rank of *professor ordinarius*

---

[16]*Holzwege*, Frankfurt a.M., 1950. Containing: "The Origin of the Work of Art" (*Der Ursprung des Kunstwerkes*, 1935-36); "The Time of the World View" (*Die Zeit des Weltbildes*, 1938); "Hegel's Notion of Experience" (*Hegels Begriff der Erfahrung*, 1942-43); "Nietzsche's Saying 'God is Dead'" (*Nietzsches Wort "Gott ist tot"*, 1936-40); "Why Poet?" (*Wozu* Dichter?, 1946); "The Maxim of Anaximander" (*Der Spruch des Anaximander*, 1946).

[17]*Einführung in die Metaphysik*, Tübingen, 1953.

[18]*Vorträge und Aufsätze*, Pfullingen, 1954. Containing: "The Question of Technique" (*Die Frage nach der Technik*, 1953); "Science and Reflection" (*Wissenschaft und Besinnung*, 1953); "Overcoming Metaphysics" (*Überwindung der Metaphysik*, 1936-46); "Who is Nietzsche's Zarathustra?" (*Wer ist Nietzsches Zarathustra?*, 1953); "What Does Thinking Mean?" (*Was heisst Denken?*, 1952); "Building, Dwelling, Thinking" (*Bauen Wohnen Denken*, 1951); "The Thing" (*Das Ding*, 1950); "Man Dwells Poetically" (". . . dichterisch wohnet der Mensch . . .", 1951); "Logos," (1951); "Moira" (1952); "Aletheia" (1943).

[19]*Was heisst Denken?*, Tübingen, 1954.

[20]"Zur Seinsfrage," *Festschrift fur Ernst Jünger*, 1955.

[21]*Was ist das—die Philosophie?*, Pfullingen, 1956.

[22]*Der Satz vom Grund*, Pfullingen, 1957.

[23]*Identität und Differenz*, Pfullingen, 1957.

[24]*Unterwegs zur Sprache*, Pfullingen, 1959.

[25]*Nietzsche*, Pfullingen, 1961.

[26]*Vom Wesen und Begriff der Physis*, Milano, 1962.

[27]Like many other German words, "Heimat" (of the same root as "Home") has no adequate equivalent in English. For a German in foreign countries, Germany is his "Heimat." Within Germany, the state, province, region, town or village where one is born or resides permanently is one's "Heimat." In addition to a mainly geographical notion, this word also has an affective connotation of belonging, of personal attachment (Tr.).

once in 1930 and again in 1933. He declined both times and tried to justify his attitude in an essay entitled, "Why Do We Stay in the Countryside?"[28] Heidegger explained in it that his deep attachment to the scenery of the Black Forest made him unable and unwilling to separate himself from it, for permanent close contact with his "Heimat" remained for him an indispensable source of thinking.

He added that he disliked the big city and its way of life. He feared that publicity, society life and all kinds of conventional obligations might interfere with original thinking about the main questions of philosophy. He expressed his longing for tranquillity, silence, solitude and familiarity with people, objects and environment, since only these made it possible to have moments of intense concentration, fundamental vision and original expression.

Thus it is not surprising that Heidegger is sometimes compared with Kant, with whom he has many other traits in common.

History and Historicity of Philosophy

Heidegger's writings give clear evidence that he is well informed about the history of philosophy. "Historical" reflections often occupy a major place in his works and he has dealt with all but a few of the great philosophers. He wrote extensively on Parmenides, Heraclitus, Plato, Aristotle, Duns Scotus, Descartes, Kant, Hegel, Nietzsche and others.

Although Heidegger manifests an excellent acquaintance with these authors, he sometimes explains their doctrines in a way that at first appears astonishing. It is not his intention, however, to write history in the strict sense of the word; even in his "historical" meditations

---

[28]*Warum bleiben wir in der Provinz?*, 1934. Quoted by Hühnerfeld, *op. cit.*, pp. 83-84.

he tries to find and to clarify the important problems with which his mind is occupied and to present his own viewpoint on these problems.

This procedure is closely linked to his notion of the historicity of human existence and of human thinking, and especially to his entirely new and unique attitude with regard to the meaning and the significance of ontology.

Linguistic Innovations

Finally a word about Heidegger's language. Reading his works is extremely difficult, and many of his own countrymen are of the opinion that he writes atrocious German. His language contains numerous individualistic peculiarities and seems to have undergone a strong influence of the regional dialect.

He likes, moreover, to use archaic expressions. And whenever the current language seems to him inadequate for the proper expression of his ideas, Heidegger forges new words in the true manner of a poet. This practice of creating entirely new words and expressions for entirely new things has often been termed presumptuous arrogance. Heidegger has sometimes been ridiculed for this; in certain circles conversation was purposely, and regardless of whether it was appropriate or inappropriate, interspersed with such expressions as "Man mans" and "The thing things."[29]

José Ortega y Gasset, however, took a more judicious attitude by distinguishing between belletristic language and philosophical terminology. Granted that Heidegger's German may be deficient from a literary point of view, and also that sometimes his inventiveness carries him too far, his choice of words nevertheless constitutes a philosophical terminology which is excellently suited for

---

[29]These expressions employ the non-existing verbs "menschen" (to man) and "dingen" (to thing), derived from the corresponding nouns (Tr.).

an adequate expression of his often very profound thoughts.

His word derivations are frequently far-fetched and they certainly are not always correct. Heidegger, to be sure, is well aware of all this. It is not his intention, however, to etymologize, but rather to give a more profound and in a way also a more original meaning to words of daily discourse.

However true this may be, these considerations about Heidegger's typical linguistic practices do not tell the whole story. His language is very closely connected with the essence of what he considers philosophy. According to Heidegger, there exists a very intimate relation between thought and language. Consequently only a well developed philosophy of language can fully explain his attitude regarding the use of words and sentences.

CHAPTER TWO

ONTOLOGICAL PERSPECTIVE
AND METHOD

1. THE QUESTION OF BEING[1]

being and Man

The task of philosophy is to reveal the last foundations of being and of our knowledge of being; from the very beginning philosophy has claimed its intention to proceed as "radically" as possible. This does not mean, however, that the philosopher wants to start from nothing or confine himself solely to the consideration of being and truth.

In addition to questions of being and truth, questions about man have always been a central theme of philosophy. What is man? Whence does he come and whither does he go? What is the exact meaning of his existence? What is his place and significance in the world? How is he related to the other-than-man and to other people? If he himself is not the ground of all that is, what is his relation to be-ings, to being, and to the ground of all that

---

[1]We will translate the German *Sein* or *das Sein* (Dutch *zijn* or *het zijn*) by "being," and the German *Seiendes* (Dutch *zijnde*) by "be-ing." Sometimes *Seiendes* has to be translated by the plural "be-ings" (cf. W. Kaufman, *Existentialism from Dostoevsky to Sartre,* New York, 1960, p. 206). We reject, however, the translation of *das Seiende* and *ein Seiendes* by "existence" and "existent" (cf. Heidegger, *Essays in Metaphysics: Identity and Difference,* tr. by Kurt F. Leidecker, New York, 1960, p. 81). We also see no need for introducing the neologism "essent" (cf. Heidegger, *An Introduction to Metaphysics,* tr. by Ralph Manheim, New York, 1961, p. xi; Heidegger, *Kant and the Problem of Metaphysics,* tr. by James S. Churchill, Bloomington, 1962, p. xv). It stands to reason that *sein* as an auxiliary verb or as the copula of a proposition is translated by forms of the verb "to be," including the present participle "being." In addition to *be-ing* and *being,* we will also use *Being.* For this term, see below Chapter 11, Section 3. (Tr).

is? For many centuries such questions have been central problems of philosophy.

Moreover, philosophy has always occupied itself with other areas, such as the things in the world, space and time, science, ethics, art and religion. In all this, however, the question What is man? is somehow always a cardinal point. Thus, on the one hand, philosophy deals foremost with being and truth while, on the other, man also occupies a fundamental place. How is it possible to bring these two statements into agreement?

Heidegger is of the opinion that one does not have to look far for the link between them, for the question What is being? is very closely related to the question How can being be reached? Therefore, the answer to the question about the meaning of being will lead us automatically to the question of what man is.

Necessity of Asking Again the Question of being

Ever since its origin, European philosophy has generally regarded the question, What is being? as its central question. However, although everybody thinks he knows what being is, and although for many centuries traditional philosophy has dealt with this fundamental question, it has to be asked again. This is due to the fact that the preliminary insights gained by the Greeks were accepted as "self-evident" and taken for granted by traditional philosophy. The problem was not restated and rethought over and again "as a thematic question for actual investigation."[2]

Consequently, many thinkers have completely forgotten the real problem of philosophy. A true philosopher will have to take up this problem again where the early Greeks, especially Parmenides and Heraclitus, left off. Otherwise he will be misled by the above-mentioned "self-evidence" and will be unaware of the heart of the question. He will

---

[2]*Sein und Zeit,* p. 2. All editions of *Sein und Zeit* are practically identical. We will refer to this work by the abbreviation *S.Z.* (Tr.)

fail to realize how empty the traditional concept of being is.[3]

Although traditional philosophy is right in stating that this concept of being is the most general one of all, it is nevertheless true that this concept implies real and fundamental problems. This concept is used in the most diverse meanings, thus it is far from being evident,[4] and therefore it should be reexamined in a systematic manner.

Such a reexamination is only possible when one already knows to some extent the proper character of what one is looking for. The way in which a question is stated already somehow implies the answer. The very fact that man asks himself the question of what being means proves that he has already some idea of what the answer is supposed to be. In reality we notice that all ordinary and normal people have such a preliminary understanding of the meaning of being.

One of the main tasks of philosophy is to purify, enlarge and assign a foundation to this preliminary insight, to eliminate its vagueness and explain the factors which have led to this vagueness.[5]

Special Difficulty of the Question About being

The main difficulty which one encounters from the start is the fact that being cannot be defined and that it is not well suited for demonstration; being simply is not a *demonstrandum,* for it cannot be dealt with from a standpoint outside being itself. Moreover, any question about being presupposes necessarily that every radical distinction between that which is investigated and the be-ing who asks about the meaning of being has to be excluded. Therefore, an adequate approach to the problem of being requires its own method, its own way of bringing to light.[6]

---

[3] *S.Z.,* p. 2.
[4] *S.Z.,* pp. 3-4.
[5] *S.Z.,* pp. 5-6.
[6] *S.Z.,* p. 6.

However, that more is needed to circumvent all difficulties should be immediately evident from the following considerations. We have already mentioned that in the last analysis philosophy always asks questions about being, for it is being which makes be-ings be-ings. Being itself, however, is not a be-ing and therefore it cannot be reduced to any be-ing. But since being is the being of be-ings, the search for an answer to the question of being has to be started from a be-ing and this be-ing has to be asked about its own being. This be-ing, in order to be able to bring to light the proper characteristics of its own being in an authentic fashion, must itself be accessible from the start as it is by and in itself.[7]

Privileged Position of Man's being (Dasein)

There are very many be-ings. All of them are rightly called be-ings, but each one of them is a be-ing in a different sense. Which be-ing ought to be selected by philosophy as the gateway leading toward the discovery of the true and proper sense of being? Can one arbitrarily choose any be-ing or is there perhaps a be-ing that occupies a privileged position with regard to our question? And if the reply is in the affirmative, which be-ing is so privileged and in what sense does it rank above all other be-ings?

At first these questions seem unanswerable; but a closer examination reveals that there is one be-ing, and one only, which could provide a firm starting point for the question about the meaning of being. This be-ing is the be-ing that can question *itself* about its own being—man himself.

Thus, only by a profound analysis of man's being or *Dasein*[8] can we arrive at an insight into the being of the

---

[7]*S.Z.*, p. 7.

[8]We follow the practice of not translating the German word *Dasein* (cf. Vincent Vycinas, *Earth and Gods,* The Hague, 1961, pp. 24-25). If this word were always used in its traditional meaning of "actual existence," as in the standard expression *der Kampf ums Dasein* (the struggle for survival), there would be no objec-

be-ings. In this sense an analysis of our human "existence"[9] constitutes a necessary condition for a genuine ontology.[10]

By selecting an analysis of *Dasein* as the starting point of metaphysics, we have put *Dasein* in a certain favored position in philosophy.[11] This privileged position is not based on philosophical prejudices, as is the case in most idealistic systems, but is imposed upon us by the very data of our problem. It does not yet imply any value judgment nor does it establish any hierarchy in the onto-

---

tion against rendering it such in English. But in addition to using it in this sense, e.g., *Dasein des Griechentums* (*Was ist das—die Philosophie?*, p. 18), Heidegger employs it first and foremost in the sense of "human *Dasein*" and as such he gives it a new and unique meaning. The various attempts at translating it cannot be considered successful. Expressions as "human being," "human existence" or even "thing-in-being called man" fail to capture the specific Heideggerian meaning of *Dasein* (cf. H. Spiegelberg, *The Phenomenological Movement*, vol. I, The Hague, 1960, p. 285, note 1). "Being-there" (cf. Heidegger, *An Introduction to Metaphysics*, tr. by Ralph Manheim, New York, 1961, pp. xi and 8) comes closer but impoverishes its content, since the German *Da* is not simply the equivalent of the English "there." *Dasein*, "Therebeing," says Richardson, "is the There of Being among beings— it lets beings *be* (manifest), thereby rendering all encounter with them possible" (*Heidegger. Through Phenomenolgy to Thought*, p. 40). (Tr.)

[9]"Heidegger introduces the term 'existence' in a sense which clearly differs from all previous usages, Scholastic as well as Kierkegaardian." (Spiegelberg, *op. cit.*, vol. I, p. 327). The scholastic meaning of this term was and is that of actuality as distinguished from essence. The meaning given to it by Kierkegaard, Jaspers and others is indicated by Heidegger with the usual adjective *existenziell*. To characterize the specific sense which this word has in his own philosophy, he coined the neologism *existenzial*. (Spiegelberg, *op. cit.*, vol. I, p. 301). An adequate translation of both terms will render the English "existentiel" for *existenziell* and "existential" for *existenzial*. The fact that the English "existential" has been used to translate *existentiell* undoubtedly leads to much confusion (cf. I. M. Bochenski, *Contemporary European Philosophy*, Berkeley, 1957, p. 163). "Existentiel" refers to the ontic dimension of existence; "existential" is used in reference to the analysis of the structural features of *Dasein's* existence (cf. *S.Z.*, p. 12). In *On the Essence of Truth* (written in 1930, but first published in 1943), Heidegger introduced a new spelling *Ek-sistenz*. This has led to the translation of *Dasein* by the English neologism "Ek-sistent" (cf. Langan, *The Meaning of Heidegger*, New York, 1959, p. 11). (Tr.)

[10]*S.Z.*, pp. 183, 7, 13, 37, 39.

[11]*S.Z.*, p. 8.

logical order. The question whether man occupies a privileged position in an ontological sense among be-ings has to be examined elsewhere.

Privileged Position of the Question of being

Dasein occupies a favored position, as we saw, in the question of being; in turn, the question of being itself occupies a privileged position compared to all other problems which man is able to raise.[12] There are several reasons for this.

First, all other problems which man encounters refer ultimately and necessarily to the question of being, so that they are subordinate to it. All sciences must inevitably start with a prescientific notion of their objects. For a while they develop without questioning or carefully examining these preliminary notions by which their pursuit has been, hitherto, more or less successfully directed. Once, however, a systematic whole has been formed, attention begins to be paid to the foundations of the sciences. As is exemplified by the case of mathematics, physics, biology, psychology and sociology, such an examination always leads to a crisis regarding these foundations. Only when such fundamental difficulties have been solved, do the sciences in question become genuinely scientific forms of knowledge. This examination of foundations consists always in a precise explicitation of a definite and special structure of being.[13]

Thus it should be evident that a complete explicitation of a particular structure of being, which a science endeavors to isolate from all other structures to make it the object of its special study, will ultimately raise the big question about the meaning of being in general. The solution of the problem about this or that structure of being remains naive and superficial as long as the question about the meaning of being in general is not asked.[14]

---

[12]*S.Z.*, p. 9.
[13]*S.Z.*, p. 10.
[14]*S.Z.*, pp. 10-11.

It is very simple to arrive at the same conclusion with regard to all problems of philosophy. The solution of every philosophical problem presupposes ultimately an answer to the question of the meaning of being in general. Thus the question of this meaning is the most fundamental and the most primordial question, no matter from which standpoint one prefers to consider it.[15]

The primacy of the problem of being and the privileged position which the study of *Dasein* occupies in solving this problem can also be shown in other ways. All sciences are man-made; therefore all scientific problems can only be raised by man. Consequently, the existence of any science presupposes the existence of man; without man there is no science. Scientific activity and generally constituting a science is a mode of being of man. It is doubtless neither the only one, nor the most ordinary one and certainly not man's most fundamental way of being.[16]

If, then, we want to arrange the problems which we can raise according to their importance, problems about a mode of being must be subordinated to the problems about the being of those be-ings whose mode of being we are examining and generally to the problems about the meaning of being as such.

Having indicated the central problem of philosophy and having shown the main road toward its solution, we must now consider the method of examination.

2. THE PHENOMENOLOGICAL METHOD

The failures which traditional ontology has suffered in this respect and the vague ideas which abound in it do not particularly invite us to have much confidence in its methods. For this reason we can hardly have recourse to the history of philosophy to help us choose a good method for the study of our difficult problem since this history itself

---

[15]*S.Z.*, p. 11.
[16]*S.Z.*, pp. 11, 15.

makes it evident that all existing methods are doubtful and unreliable.

It would not be advisable to adopt any method *a priori* anyhow, for we should let ourselves be guided by the things themselves which appear to us immediately. The character and features of the things which we are to study spontaneously indicate which method we should use. Because this procedure is the fundamental principle of phenomenology, we may say that phenomenology can perhaps provide an appropriate method for ontology.

"Back to the Things Themselves"

First we must describe what is meant by phenomenology. Obviously, however, this description can only be provisional, and further research will have to give it a more concrete content.[17]

Phenomenology indicates primarily a principle of method, which can best be formulated in Husserl's phrase: "Back to the things themselves." This expression does not mean that one should return to naive realism; but it indicates that in philosophy one should renounce all principles and ideas that are insufficiently explained or incorrectly founded, all arbitrary ways of thinking and all prejudices, and be guided only by the things themselves. Of course, philosophy does not intend to stop with the description of what immediately manifests itself to us. It intends to penetrate, by way of what shows itself immediately, to that which at first is still hidden and which constitutes the meaning and ground of what is immediately manifest. This is in the last instance the being of be-ings.[18]

Etymologically, phenomenology (*legein ta phainomena*) means "science of phenomena." Throughout the history of philosophy, the term "phenomenon" has been given many senses, but these meanings have no importance for us here. Phenomenon here refers to everything that

---

[17]*S.Z.*, p. 27.
[18]*S.Z.*, p. 35.

shows itself to us, in whatever form this may be. To show itself here does not mean merely to appear to the senses; a feeling, a work of art, a political institution, a philosophical idea—all these show themselves just as real to us as a color or sound, though in quite a different way. Moreover, that which shows itself does not have to appear to everyone; even my states of consciousness show themselves to me, so that they too can be objects of phenomenological analysis and description. In addition, one should keep in mind that phenomenology does not want to oppose that which shows itself to that which does not show itself. In other words, that which shows itself to us immediately is not to be taken as a correct or incorrect representative of a thing in itself that remains essentially hidden. Hence the Kantian sense of phenomenon has to be rejected also.

Although it is true that a first examination of phenomena discovers characteristics which do not immediately manifest themselves to us, this does not mean that the initial phenomenon is a sign of something that cannot appear itself. On the contrary, everything "which already shows itself in the appearance as prior to the 'phenomenon' in the ordinary [i.e., the Kantian] sense and as accompanying it in every case, can, even though it thus shows itself unthematically, be brought to show itself thematically; and what thus shows itself in itself . . . will be the 'phenomena' of phenomenology."[19]

If the idea of a phenomenon as described above is connected with the idea expressed by the verb *legein* in the sense of "to let appear," phenomenology can be said to be a precise method which intends to let everything which shows itself to us appear to us in a clear way, as it shows itself to us.[20]

---

[19] *S.Z.*, p. 31.
[20] *S.Z.*, p. 34.

No "Bracketing of being"

The transcendental phenomenological reduction or *epoché,* as the "bracketing of being," is of special importance in Husserl's phenomenology.[21] Although Husserl's ideas underwent development on this point, he always maintained the *epoché* in his published works. It even seems that its meaning grew and became more widespread rather than narrower. It will not be surprising to learn that Heidegger explicitly dismisses this reduction. He wants to make the being of be-ings the explicit object of a completely new ontology, which he intends to create through the phenomenological method. For this reason it is obvious that he has no interest in the "bracketing of being." That which Husserl regarded as a necessary condition for philosophy as a rigorous science, is for Heidegger the negation of an authentic philosophical attitude. In this sense, therefore, these two thinkers seem to be very far apart.

Any phenomenon presents, according to Heidegger, a suitable starting point for a philosophical reflection. But this does not mean that certain phenomena are not especially suitable for such a reflection. Heidegger does not pursue phenomenology for its own sake but wants to use it only to support an ontology. Therefore, Heidegger's phenomenology is only interested in those phenomena that have a special meaning from his standpoint, that is, those that are able to enlighten us about the being of be-ings. But the being of be-ings does not appear immediately. Although the being of be-ings constitutes the meaning and foundation of that which appears immediately, this being usually remains hidden.[22] Since the being of be-ings is usually not immediately manifest, it has to be dis-closed, "un-concealed." This, according to Heidegger, is the primary task of phenomenology.[23]

---

[21] The *epoché* or "bracketing" refers to the suspension of judgment with respect to something. The "bracketing of being" means to suspend judgment regarding real existence. (Tr.)

[22] *S.Z.*, p. 35.

[23] *S.Z.*, p. 37.

Ontology and Phenomenology

On reading such statements, one can inquire how a philosopher who wishes to employ a descriptive method can substantiate and justify his right to state that the foundation of the phenomena generally remains hidden at first. It is also difficult to see how one can justify, from the standpoint of phenomenology, the distinction between what is fundamental and what is not. Even if one can subsequently demonstrate that such a distinction is founded, how can it be referred to prior to any phenomenological analysis? The striking difference between the standpoint of Husserl and that of Heidegger regarding the meaning of phenomenology becomes clear again by reflection on these questions.

For Husserl, phenomenology is not only a completely autonomous science, but it is also the only science which can absolutely and radically found all its statements independently from any other science or scientific method. For this reason phenomenology is for Husserl *the* philosophy and, if it makes sense to speak of metaphysics or ontology, then this metaphysics or this ontology is either phenomenology itself or only a system of conclusions which of necessity results from phenomenology. According to Husserl therefore, ontology derives its object, problems and everything that is needed to solve them from phenomenology, while phenomenology constitutes itself independently from an ontology or a metaphysics.

For Heidegger, however, the relations between ontology and phenomenology are entirely different. Heidegger is quite sceptical of the value which Husserl ascribes to pure analysis and description. To him, phenomenology is not the root and source of the whole philosophy, but solely the instrument of a pre-existing but still implicit doctrine. We will have to return to this point later. Confining ourselves to the questions with which we have confronted Heidegger, we may say that Heidegger can defend his viewpoint by referring to the history of philosophy and to the necessity of a reduction from a cultural world to a "lived world" and by referring to some other points which can only be considered in the analysis of *Dasein*.

Anyhow, according to Heidegger the real object of the phenomenological analysis and description consists in bringing to light those elements which initially are still hidden but which, in fact, are precisely the foundation of the immediately manifest traits of what shows itself to us. We must even say that the features which at the outset remain concealed are the proper, even the exclusive, object of phenomenology correctly understood: "The phenomenological conception of 'phenomenon' regards the being of be-ings, its meaning, its modifications and derivatives as that which shows itself."[24] But that which is at first concealed is not to be understood as an absolutely unapproachable "thing in itself" in the sense of Kant.

All this, of course, does not exhaust Heidegger's idea of phenomenology nor his vision of ontology. It seems to suffice, however, for the correct understanding of Heidegger's fundamental intentions. The aim of *Being and Time,* and of all his subsequent writings, is to offer a philosophy of being. The analysis of human existence is only a necessary preliminary study. For this reason it is evident that it is incorrect to rank Heidegger among the existentialists —he even has expressly protested against this. "I must . . . say again that my philosophical tendencies . . . can not be classified as a philosophy of existence. . . . The question which preoccupies me is not the question of human existence, but it is the question of being as a whole and as such."[25] Whether Heidegger has really succeeded in developing an ontology in this sense, will have to be investigated later. The same must be said about the question whether phenomenology as described by him is by itself sufficient to arrive at such an ontology.

---

[24]*S.Z.,* p. 35.
[25]*Bulletin de la Société française de philosophie,* vol. XXXVII, no. 5, p. 193.

CHAPTER THREE

BEING-IN-THE-WORLD—THE WORLDHOOD OF THE WORLD

1. MAN'S BEING-IN-THE-WORLD

Directedness to the World

Originally Heidegger intended to divide *Being and Time* into two large parts. In the first part an interpretation of man's being was to be given with emphasis on the temporality of *Dasein*. He also wanted to show in this part that time had to be conceived as the transcendental limit for the question of the meaning of being. The second part would then critically examine the history of ontology, on the basis of the insights acquired in the first part, with special attention to the works of Kant, Descartes and Aristotle.

Actually, however, only the interpretation of man's being has been published. The question regarding the relation between being and time remains unanswered, as well as the problems which Heidegger wanted to discuss in the second part in connection with the history of ontology. In works published after *Being and Time,* Heidegger has returned to different problems which he had intended to consider in *Being and Time.*

Later we will return to the question why the last portion of the first part as well as the whole second part of *Being and Time* have never been published. At present we will limit ourselves to the interpretation of man's being as it is found in the first part of *Being and Time.* It is important to stress once again that these considerations have to be read in an ontological perspective: their purpose is to prepare an answer to the question regarding the meaning of being.[1]

---

[1] *S.Z.*, pp. 39-40.

Heidegger expresses the mode of being proper to man, which makes man man, in the term "existence" (*Existenz*), i.e., "standing out toward," because it is peculiar to man that, in order to realize himself, man has to "come out" of himself. Man is primordially and essentially directed to the world and therefore each manifestation of his being-man is a way to relate himself actively to the world. Man is primordially and essentially an intentional and self-transcending be-ing. Only through his familiarity with the world does man become himself. His being is being-in-the-world.

Since this being-in-the-world is the first and fundamental feature which we encounter as we look at *Dasein,* the analysis of human existence has to start with the explanation of being-in-the-world. From this first and fundamental relation we should try to understand all other characteristics of *Dasein.*[2] The expresssion "being-in-the-world" indicates a single primordial phenomenon which contains a plurality of constitutive, structural moments. A thorough examination of these structural elements of being-in-the-world will allow us to clarify the genuine meaning of the mode of being proper to man. These elements are 1) *"being in,"* 2) the *being* of the be-ing that is in the world, and 3) the *world* in which this be-ing is. As we will see, a careful analysis of the first element will lead us to the second and the third.

"Being in"

The preposition "in" usually indicates a relation of the contained to the container; for example, the chair is in the room and the room is in the house. *Dasein* evidently is not in the world in the same way as a match is in a box. With respect to the match, the preposition "in" merely indicates a spatial relation between two or more be-ings; but in the expression "being-in-the-world," the

---

[2]*S.Z.*, pp. 52-53.

particle "in" indicates that man's being can be understood only through *Dasein's* essential relationship to the
world. Without the organized and structured other-than-
man, which we call "the world," *Dasein* can neither be
nor be understood. Hence, when we say that *Dasein*
means being-in-the-world, this statement does not merely
express an actual situation, but wants to say something
regarding *Dasein's* own being itself, which cannot be
without this essential relation to the other.

Instead of referring to a spatial relation, the preposition
"in" indicates a familiarity "with" and a being "with."
"In" as well as "with" expresses that *Dasein* is acquainted
with something, is used to something, is conversant with
something, and that it takes this "something" to heart.
This, of course, does not mean that one should not accept
a certain spatiality for *Dasein*. There certainly is such a
spatiality, and we will have to speak about it later. At
present we merely want to say that the expressions "being
in" and "being with" must be understood in the above-
mentioned sense.[3]

Dasein's "being in" can take many different forms, all
of which could be analyzed phenomenologically. All these
modalities, however, appear to be concrete ways of a fundamental form of "being in" which Heidegger calls "concern"
(*Besorgen*). Like "being in" and "being-in-the-world,"
this "being concerned" is also an existentiale, i.e., a fundamental and constitutive element of the basic structure of
the being proper to *Dasein*.[4] The transcendental relationship of Dasein to the world thus assumes primarily
and primordially the form of "being concerned." For this
reason an accurate study of the primordial concern will be
a suitable guide toward a total interpretation of man's own
being. Before continuing our analysis of "being in" we
will, therefore, have to say something about concern. Since,
however, this question about the characteristics of concern

---

[3]*S.Z.*, pp. 52-56.
[4]*S.Z.*, p. 57.

is connected with the problem of the world, we will have to start with that.[5]

2. The World. Introduction

Dasein and World

It is very difficult to answer the question of what the world is. A first but very superficial answer is obtained by enumerating all the things that are in the "world." It stands to reason, however, that one will never succeed in saying what the world really is by assuming that the world obviously is the sum total of all be-ings in the world.

One could, of course, go about it more systematically by distinguishing different domains of be-ings, determining which of these is the most fundamental domain, and trying to explain its properties. Even this, however, would not lead to an insight into the essence of the world, not even if one uses the data gathered by the modern sciences. For the proper character of things is known from the world and not the world from things.

If, then, the world cannot be understood as a characteristic of things because things presuppose the world, is it perhaps possible to discover what the world is in its own being by considering it as a characteristic of *Dasein's* own being?[6] This question, of course, does not immediately eliminate all difficulties, for this change of viewpoint raises a whole series of questions. Is the world not ultimately a determination of the be-ing that does *not* belong to the order of *Dasein?* But in that case how can this be-ing be defined as intraworldly be-ing? Is the world then perhaps nonetheless an existentiale of *Dasein?* But doesn't it follow then that each *Dasein* has its own world? Does not the world become something subjective? How can there still be a common world in which we all live? And if we raise the question about *the* world, what world do we have in

[5]*S.Z.*, p. 63.
[6]*S.Z.*, p. 64.

mind? Neither the common nor the subjective world, but rather the worldhood of the world as such. How does one meet this worldhood?

In these suggestive questions Heidegger's intentions begin to assume more concrete form. The real problem here is the worldhood of the world, i.e., that which constitutes the world as such, regardless of whether it is my world, your world or our world. These questions also indicate that the "world" is not to be taken as a sum of things, but as another structural element of *Dasein's* definition. Heidegger's "world" here has what he calls an ontologico-existential meaning.

The Distinction Ontological-Ontic

The distinction between ontological and ontic is derived from the distinction between being and be-ing. One can regard a be-ing simply as it is. This is the ontic standpoint: it has to do with the Greek *on,* the *ens,* be-ing. But one can also try to understand the being of be-ings, that which makes this be-ing be what it is, its fundamental and constituent structure. In this case one does not stop with be-ing as it is immediately given, but one tries to understand be-ing *as* be-ing, that is, the proper being of this be-ing, in short its being. This is the ontological order. In his later works Heidegger also distinguishes between the being of be-ings and Being, and refers to the former as the "be-ingness" (*Seiendheit*) of be-ings.

Meanings of the World

By saying that the notion "world" has an ontologico-existential meaning, he wants to indicate that he does not intend to limit his search to a description of what man ordinarily calls "world," but wants to dis-cover its essential structure, its being. He also wants to express that this structure is founded on human existence: "Ontologically 'world' is not a way of characterizing the be-ings which *Dasein* essentially is not; but it is rather a character-

istic of *Dasein* itself."[7] Worldhood is in itself an ontological concept because it indicates the structure of a constituent moment of being-in-the-world, which itself is an
existential definition of *Dasein*. If we inquire about the
world in this perspective, we consider it in an ontologico-
existential way, so that the term "world" has an ontologico-
existential meaning.[8]

In this way Heidegger shows us the direction in which
he wants to look for a solution of the problem regarding
the world. In his attempt to explain and justify his viewpoint, Heidegger starts by accurately circumscribing the
different meanings which the term "world" can assume:

1. As an ontic term, "world" signifies the totality of
be-ings which can be present within the "universe."[9]

2. As an ontological term it means the being of the
world as the totality of be-ings. In a derivative form
"world" can also be used in this sense in reference to a
particular realm encompassing a particular group of be-
ings; for instance, the "world" of the mathematician or
the "world" of the scientist.

3. "World" can signify that "wherein" *Dasein* concretely lives, my personal world or our common world.
Here the term "world" is again taken in an ontic sense,
because it refers to *Dasein* as be-ing insofar as no effort
has yet been made to bring the intrinsic structure of
Dasein to light. In this case Heidegger speaks of a "pre-
ontological," concrete-existentiel meaning of the "world."
Let us explain what he means.

Dasein, as existing, necessarily implies a certain relation
to, and a knowledge of, its own being. This knowledge
which to *Dasein* as existing is essential, however, is not
yet explicit and thematic, and for this reason Heidegger

[7] *S.Z.*, p. 64.
[8] *S.Z.*, p. 64.
[9] *S.Z.*, p. 64.

calls it a pre-ontological understanding. Moreover, *Dasein* as existing is being-in-the-world, but since this being-in-the-world is taken here only as a concrete fact, this understanding of *Dasein's* own being and therefore also this understanding of the world is a pre-ontological existentiel understanding. If one would have understood *Dasein* here according to its essential structure and not just as a concrete fact, this understanding would have been called "existential" and not "concrete-existentiel."

4. In its ontologico-existential sense "world" means the worldhood, which is the object of the present inquiry.[10] This sense is ontological because it explicitly and thematically aims at the structure of being-in-the-world and it is existential insofar as it is to be understood as a structural element of *Dasein*. In contrast to *Dasein,* which he calls "worldly," Heidegger refers to intraworldly be-ings as "belonging to the world" (*weltzugehörig*). Hence the terms "intraworldly" and "belonging to the world" indicate the distinguishing features of the presence of things in the world to man.[11]

Surveying the history of philosophy regarding the views taken of the world, one notices that the world has never been understood as a structural moment of *Dasein*. The reason lies in the fact that *Dasein* itself has never been regarded as being-in-the-world. When the problem of the world is considered, it is usually restricted to a certain group of intraworldly be-ings, for instance, nature— although even nature has never been discovered explicitly as such. Anyhow, nature, as studied by physics, is considered to be the basis of the other domains of be-ings, which, in contrast to the domain of nature, are called the domain of values. As we will see later, such a conception of nature as the basis of all other be-ings can only arise through a change of *Dasein's* primordial viewpoint with

---

[10]*S.Z.*, p. 65.
[11]*S.Z.*, pp. 64-65.

respect to the world, a change through which the world is deprived of its worldhood. At any rate, nature as the categorical aggregate of certain structures of being possessed by a certain group of intraworldly be-ings cannot possibly explain the worldhood of the world.[12]

3. The Being of Intraworldly be-ings

Concern

Before a positive answer can be given to the question of the being proper to the world, we must first speak about the being proper to intraworldly be-ings. Our everyday existence is, according to Heidegger, characterized by "concern," our dealings with intraworldly be-ings. In those dealings *Dasein* is not primarily interested in mere knowledge but in action, in manipulating things and putting them to use. Our theoretical knowledge is only a derived mode of this primordial concernful being-in-the-world.[13]

Let us now limit ourselves provisionally to the question of how exactly intrawordly be-ings are present to *Dasein* in its concernful dealing with things. For this purpose we must carefully analyze and describe our concernful dealing with intraworldly be-ings. It is difficult to describe the phenomenon of concern correctly because of the obstacles created by all kinds of prejudice which we have already formed in our everyday life.[14]

Moreover, one could also object that such an analysis would be a waste of time because it obviously deals with matters that everybody knows already. What could be more trivial than knowing that in our daily concern we deal with things? However, this objection takes for granted that we know what precisely makes a thing a thing. In what does the thinghood of a thing really consist? Some think that it lies in the reality or materiality

---

[12]*S.Z.*, pp. 65-66.
[13]*S.Z.*, pp. 59-62.
[14]*S.Z.*, p. 67.

of things, which could be further explained through extension; for others, things are "objects of value." Yet the things which we encounter in our everyday concernful dealings clearly do not appear to us as material objects or as objects of value. Starting from either view leads to overlooking the typical character of things.

Equipment

Greek thought was more primordial than ours because the Greeks were closer to that which primordially appeared to man. The old Greeks spoke about *pragmata* in reference to that which one has to do with in one's *praxis,* one's concernful dealing with things. Going back to the Greeks, Heidegger calls everything we encounter in our everyday concern "equipment," "gear" (*Zeug*). In this sense we still speak of equipment or gear for fishing, working or playing in reference to the things used "in order to" fish, work or play. Thus everything that in any way serves "in order to . . ." will be called "equipment" from now on. The question, then, is, What is typical, proper and characteristic of equipment, what is the "equipmentness" of equipment, that which makes equipment equipment?

Equipment is never by itself, but is always and solely in reference to other equipment. What constitutes this equipment manifold precisely as unity? Each separate piece of equipment is something "in order to . . .," it "serves to. . . ." The various modalities of this "serving to" characterize the "what . . . for," the meaning of the equipment. Thus the various pieces of equipment are connected by their "what . . . for"; and this "what . . . for" gives the equipment manifold unity.[15] "Serving to" necessarily includes a reference and assignment to something else.

In order to make progress with our analysis we must therefore consider first a concrete equipment manifold

---

[15] *S.Z.,* p. 68.

and pay special attention to the totality of the mutual references. Heidegger himself takes a room as an example. Each piece of equipment in the room is as such defined through its reference to other pieces of equipment. Moreover, one does not meet first the separate pieces of equipment and then add them up in order to construct the room from them as a unity, but one first encounters the room as such. Only in and through this totality do the separate things receive their proper meaning. Our knowledge of the room does not have to be explicit or theoretical, for a certain preknowledge of what the term "room" designates is sufficient to understand what is present in the room.

Accordingly, a particular piece of equipment does not show itself and cannot be understood without the equipment manifold to which it belongs; this manifold has to be previously discovered.

"Circumspection"

The terms "to know" and "to understand" refer here to that knowledge which is still completely and immediately related to our being-concerned itself. For example, one uses a hammer in the right way without explicitly understanding the proper mode of being of this piece of equipment. In our everyday life we do not know the hammer theoretically as "simply given" and "merely there," but we know how to use it. By using the hammer in the right way within a certain equipment manifold, *Dasein* has appropriated it in the most suitable way, for a hammer is not there to be looked at, but to hammer with. By using the hammer, *Dasein,* in its everyday concernful dealing with things, has to submit to the assignment that is constituent of this piece of equipment, namely, its "what. . . for." By using the hammer, *Dasein* discovers its manipulability (*Handlichkeit*), which term clearly indicates the hammer's relationship to the hand (*manus*). A piece of equipment is a thing that is "ready to hand" (*zuhanden*); it possesses "readiness to hand": "The kind of being which equipment possesses—in which it manifests itself in its own terms—we call 'readiness to hand'."[16] The fact that each piece of equipment can be used "in order to. . ." gives it its own being, its own character, its "in itself" (*An-sich*).

By saying that our ordinary knowledge of pieces of equipment and materials is not theoretical knowledge which later somehow would be changed into practical knowledge, we do not intend to state that our everyday concernful dealing with intraworldy be-ings does not imply a standpoint and view regarding this equipment. On the contrary, our concern really includes a certain view of the equipment which immediately discovers the fundamental assignment of each piece of equipment, its peculiar reference to its "what. . . for." Our concernful dealing with things uses the piece of equipment according to the reference which manifests itself in its "serving to," its "being good for," its usability. Heidegger calls this view which *Dasein* has regarding equipment "circumspection" (*Umsicht*). Circumspection is *Dasein's* overall view of the being proper to the things around us that help us to make or to realize a piece of work, in which precisely their "what. . . for" is discovered.

The Primordial Character of Being "Ready to Hand"

The proper character of equipment, its "readiness to hand," is not explicitly evident in our everyday concernful dealing with things. In its concern *Dasein* is not primarily occupied with the equipment itself but with the piece of work that will be produced by it. It is the work to be done that makes man go to the above-mentioned referential totality; the work itself is present first.[17] But the work whose realization is previously projected itself also has the characteristic of being equipment insofar as it also is "meant for. . ." and serves to. . .".

---

[16] *S.Z.*, p. 69.
[17] *S.Z.*, p. 70.

In the piece of work we do not only discover a constitutive reference to its "what...for," its usability, but also a reference to the material which *Dasein* uses, a reference to the "whereof" (*woraus*). A table is made of wood or iron and as such refers us to "nature." Thus nature is primordially discovered in the piece of work as the material of which it is made; nature is always co-discovered in the referential totality.

Later, of course, nature can also be the theme of a special consideration, but it primarily appears in our everyday dealings with things, namely, in its necessary relation to equipment; the field, the woods, the hill stand first in function of the equipment of our daily concern: the fields are there for wheat, the forest for timber, and the hills for grapes. Finally, each piece of equipment and each piece of work refers also to *Dasein* for which it exists as such; work is there for me, for us, for all.

The important point in this consideration is that in our everyday concernful dealings things do not appear first as a kind of pure world stuff, as "raw" be-ings which subsequently would somehow receive a "form" of a "subjective" coloring. Things appear primordially as "ready to hand." A sign of this is that when we meet something new we always ask immediately what it is for. We put ourselves always in a perspective that immediately reveals to us fundamental references to tools and materials. In our everyday life we are first of all concernful. Of course, we can later change our perspective and regard the things only as "merely there" (*bloss Vorhanden*) by abstracting them from the references that are constituent for equipment. But in that case, we must first change our primordial attitude toward things. The primordial characteristic of being "ready to hand" of intraworldly be-ings is not an invention of philosophy, but indicates the being proper to equipment "in itself."

4. THE WORLDLY CHARACTER OF THE ENVIRONMENT. REFERENCE AND SIGN

The Intraworldly Character of Things in the World

What , one may ask, has all this to do with the question of the world's being? First of all, it should be evident that the world itself cannot possibly be an intraworldly be-ing. On the contrary, the world is precisely that what makes all intraworldly be-ings as such possible, for it is always presupposed by them.

What then is the being proper to the world and in what way is there a world? If *Dasein* is fundamentally being-in-the-world and always implies an understanding of its own being, then it seems to follow that *Dasein* has also necessarily a certain understanding of the world. Hence, by analyzing *Dasein* as being-in-the-world in its relation with intraworldly be-ings, it must be possible to understand something of the world "wherein" our everyday concernful dealing with things occur.

Such an anaysis demands that we first elucidate the intraworldly character of these be-ings more sharply. The traditional conceptions that start from things as "simply given" are deficient here too. Their defect is that they take off from presuppositions, while giving the appearance that they do not presuppose anything. The "simply given" thing is not primordially given, but a reduced and abstract be-ing: it is a piece of equipment which by abstraction is reduced to an object of theoretical knowledge. Of course, this knowledge is also a way of being-in-the-world, but it is not the primordial way. Our primordial way of being-in-the-world is our dealing with things in our everyday concern.[18]

"Ready to Hand" as "Merely There"

The intraworldly character of things in the world manifests itself most clearly when the equipmental order is disturbed. This can happen in three ways.

---

[18]*S.Z.*, pp. 71-72.

First, a piece of equipment can become unusable, so that it is no longer good for what it was originally meant to serve. We become aware of this, in the first place, in our concernful dealing itself and by understanding what is immediately connected with our concern. The thing that has become unusable draws attention, and its pure "being there" now becomes *conspicuous*.[19] It has lost its equipmental character and asks for repair or replacement so that it can be "ready to hand" again.

Secondly, when a piece of equipment that should be there appears to be missing, the pieces that are there become *obtrusive*. Through the absence of the one the others also become unusable; they also are no longer "ready to hand" but appear as "merely given" and "being there."

Thirdly, it can also happen that a piece of equipment that was lost suddenly reappears and by its presence asks *Dasein* to produce a certain piece of work. If this is impossible now since *Dasein* is already busy with something else, the equipment can then become disturbingly *obstinate,* an obsession to *Dasein*.

In all these cases a be-ing that, strictly speaking, should be "ready to hand" appears to us as "merely given" as merely "being there." At such moments *Dasein* becomes clearly aware of the special character of the "ready to hand": that which is conspicuous as unusable, that which is obtrusive through the absence of something else, and that which is obstinate in presenting itself at a moment when it cannot be used, can be conceived as "merely given" only in function of a more primordial "readiness to hand."[20]

As we have seen above, the being proper to the equipment with which we deal in our everyday concern must be determined through reference. On closer examination, however, it appears that our concern is not primarily

[19] *S.Z.*, p. 73.
[20] *S.Z.*, pp. 73-74.

oriented toward this referential character; it uses it without explicitly aiming at it. The referential character comes to the fore only in special cases. In our everyday concern this referential character is recognized, but the ontological structure of equipment is explicitly understood only in reflective thinking. What is implicitly experienced can be made explicit. In this explicitation, the worldhood of the world must finally come to light.[21]

The worldly character of equipment manifests itself clearly only when an unusable piece of equipment begins to appear as "merely given," i.e., at the moment when the equipment is deprived of its worldly character. This fact clearly shows that the world cannot be a sum of things. Generally speaking, one can state that the references which are constitutive for *Dasein's* world cannot be thematically and explicitly understood by a *Dasein* which is absorbed in its concernful dealing with things. If one wants to meet that which is "ready to hand" as it is "in itself," then it should precisely not be obtrusive and not conspicuous. This non-obtrusiveness and inconspicuousness are negative expressions for positive aspects of the "ready to hand." What constitutes the equipment as it is "in itself" is the fact that it is daily "ready to hand" without emerging from the referential whole of its being "in itself" as a "merely given be-ing."

However, if the world can appear in concern, then it must have been discovered previously to *Dasein* in some way. For, if the meeting of *Dasein* with what is "ready to hand" is to be possible, then the world must already have been discovered. Thus the world appears explicitly as that "wherein" *Dasein* already was and to which it later also can return explicitly. *Dasein* cannot encounter equipment save insofar as the equipment already belongs to *Dasein's* world, for the "ready to hand" would be meaningless if it were not interwoven with this worldly structure. Accordingly, *Dasein* in its "circumspective" concern

---

[21]*S.Z.,* p. 75.

operates in a totality of equipmental references, and this circumspective concern presupposes a certain familiarity with the world. How is this familiarity possible and how can the worldly character of intraworldly be-ings be explained by it?[22] It is necessary to study more accurately the phenomenon of reference in order to answer these questions.

Reference and Signs

As we have seen above, any piece of equipment has meaning only within a totality of references, and it has become clear also, but only in a sketchy way, that there must be a relation between this referential totality and the world. There must be a way from the phenomenon of reference to the worldhood of the world. In order to show more clearly the referential character proper to equipment, one can best contemplate a piece of equipment in which two references are present at the same time, for instance, the turn-signal of a car. Just as any other equipment, this red light has a constitutive reference which justifies its existence within a certain referential whole. This reference is that which makes the light suitable for signalling. Its being suitable for, its "what for," is the ontologico-categorical determination of the being proper to any piece of equipment. But by indicating the direction which the car wants to take, the signal as signal, through the act of indicating itself, creates a new reference.

Thus we have two references here: the first is fundamental and constitutive for the signal as a piece of equipment, while the second is based on the first and characterizes the ontic determination of the signal as signal. Heidegger calls the constitutive reference "serviceability for" (*Dienlichkeit*) while we can name the second one "indication."

In general one can state that the sign takes a privileged position among the other pieces of equipment in everyday

22*S.Z.*, p. 76.

concern. A sign, such as a turn-signal, has meaning neither in itself nor in merely indicating a direction, but in establishing a certain order in the world of communications. By signs and signals the world around us becomes surveyable; we can orient ourselves in the complex whole of equipment because these signs introduce a certain order in it. "A sign is not a thing which has an indicative relationship to another thing; it is rather a piece of equipment which explicitly raises an equipmental whole into our circumspection so that together with it the worldly character of the 'ready to hand' announces itself."[23] "A sign is something ontically 'ready to hand,' which as this particular piece of equipment functions at the same time as something that indicates the ontological structure of 'readiness to hand,' of referential whole and of worldhood."[24]

In what sense, we must ask, is reference the foundation of what is "ready to hand" and how can it be constitutive of worldhood in general?

5. Destination and Significance. The Worldhood of the World

Destination

The "ready to hand" always manifests itself as an intraworldly be-ing, as a be-ing belonging to the world. That which determines the "ready to hand" as such, its "readiness to hand," therefore, has somehow a relationship to the world and its worldhood. Moreover, as we have seen above, whenever we encounter anything, the world itself has been discovered previously. As pre-discovered, it precedes the discovery of individual be-ings.

The question now is How can the world let the "ready to hand" be encountered as such?[25] We already know two modes of reference: the serviceability of equipment and

---

[23]*S.Z.*, p. 80.
[24]*S.Z.*, p. 82.
[25]*S.Z.*, p. 83.

the usability of materials. The "in order to" of serviceability and the "what . . . for" of usability always determine the possible ways in which the fundamental reference, proper to any piece of equipment as such, can be
made concrete. Usually these concretizations are called
"properties"; for example, we say that an arrow has the
property of being able to indicate something and that a
stone has the property that one can use it in building a
house. However, this is not a correct way of speaking:
"merely given be-ings" have properties, but the "ready to
hand" has appropriateness and suitabilities. The appropriateness of a piece of equipment determines its properties;
thus the suitability of the hammer for hammering determines the form and the weight of its head and handle.

We also have to distinguish between serviceability and
appropriateness; serviceability is the necessary condition
for the appropriateness of equipment. The reference or
assignment of the hammer determines appropriateness and
suitability, and the latter determine its properties. A
thing is "suitable for . . ." because, as "ready to hand,"
it is determined by the "in order to . . ." of its serviceability. Serviceability and suitability therefore are related
to each other as necessary condition and concrete realization. The being proper to the "ready to hand" is thus
characterized by a referential structure, it has in itself the
character of "being relative to. . . ." For example, the
hammer is essentially relative to, involved in, hammering.
This being relative is not a secondary or accidental characteristic of the "ready to hand," but defines precisely its
essence. Heidegger calls this "being essentially relative
to . . ." *Bewandtnis,* which we may translate by "being
destined" or "destination."

This destination includes that which is destined for and
that for which something is destined. Through the destination one can adequately determine the being proper to
something that is "ready to hand."[26] The destination im-

---

[26]*S.Z.,* p. 84.

plies something that is destined for, namely, the piece of
equipment or the material, as well as that "for which" it
is destined, namely, the work that is to be done with it.
The hammer is destined for hammering; the hammering
can be destined for making furniture, the furniture for
holding books, the books for reading, and so on. The
"what . . . for" of a piece of equipment is ultimately determined by the total of all these partial destinations. Since
an infinite series of destinations is impossible, there must
be a last "what . . . for" that is no longer destined for anything else. This last "what . . . for" can only be *Dasein*
itself. *Dasein* is the ultimate "what . . . for" in which all
references included in destination find their final term.
Dasein in its concern discovers intraworldy be-ing as having a certain destination.

"Letting Be"

Heidegger calls this form of *Dasein's* discovering of
intraworldly be-ings *Bewendenlassen,* that is, "letting be
destined" or briefly "letting be," making possible and
permitting the encounter with be-ings. In order that the
intraworldly be-ing can be "ready to hand," *Dasein* must
first discover its destination within a given totality of
destinations. In this way *Dasein* does not produce the
being of equipment, but only unveils it; thus, "letting be"
is a necessary condition for the encounter with be-ing as
"ready to hand."

This "letting be" can take place in different spheres
and each time a particular kind of destination of the intraworldly be-ing appears. In the sciences it leads us to a
be-ing whose kind of destination is totally different from
the "letting be" of our everyday concern. In any case,
be-ing is never first discovered as "raw" be-ing, as a thing;
it manifests itself primordially as a be-ing with a certain
destination and it can manifest itself only with this destination once the latter has been discovered by *Dasein's* "letting
be."

Accordingly, the being proper to the "ready to hand" is its being "destined for." If this being is to be discovered, the totality of destinations proper to the multitude of intraworldly be-ings of which this equipment is a part, must have been discovered previously. Precisely this pre-discovery of a complex of destinations brings to light the worldly character of be-ings. But this is not all: the discovery of the complex of destinations which must lead to the discovery of the final "what . . . for," is ultimately based on a fundamental intention of *Dasein;* in this "that for which" (*Woraufhin*), *Dasein* discovers its world. This fundamental intention opens the domain "wherein" *Dasein* unveils the constitutive references of equipment, thereby discovering the intraworldly be-ing and freeing it as such.[27]

Significance and Worldhood

Dasein itself must be characterized essentially by a certain understanding of being in *Dasein's* own being itself. On the other hand, *Dasein* is essentially being-in-the-world. But in that case *Dasein* always already has a certain understanding of the world. This understanding of the world, as considered above, can be explained as follows: "That wherein *Dasein* understands itself beforehand in the mode of referring itself is 'that for which' it has let be-ings be encountered beforehand. The 'wherein' of an act of understanding which refers itself is 'that for which' one lets be-ings be encountered in the kind of being that belongs to destinations; and this 'wherein' is the phenomenon of the world. And the structure of 'that to which' *Dasein* assigns and refers itself is what makes up the worldhood of the world."[28]

Heidegger's "wherein" should not be understood here in a spatial sense. The term merely indicates the "being with" and "being open to" which are essential to *Dasein*.

[27] *S.Z.*, p. 86.
[28] *S.Z.*, p. 86.

By remaining within the references which this "wherein" includes, *Dasein* discovers the destination of the intra-worldly be-ings, their being "ready to hand." At the same time *Dasein* discovers its being as a potentiality for being insofar as it learns to understand its own existence by grasping the references as *a priori* conditions and foundations of its own activities. For this reason one could also speak about the referential character of all the references included in the "wherein" as "signifying" (*bedeuten*). If the totality of all signifying relations is called significance, then this term can be suitably used to indicate the worldhood of the world, the essential structure of that "wherein" *Dasein* is existent.

All this enables us to have a better understanding of *Dasein's* being-in-the-world. In its familiarity with the context of references to which it itself contributes and which determine the proper character of the world, *Dasein* is the ontic condition for the possibility of discovering the intraworldly be-ing. This be-ing, as being "ready to hand," is always encountered in that world and can thus make itself known as it is in itself.[29] *Dasein* is in this way defined as such: along with its own being, a context of "ready to hand" things is essentially co-discovered. *Dasein,* insofar as it is what it is, has always related itself already to a world which it encounters, and this reference to and dependence on such a world belongs essentially to *Dasein's* being. The context of references itself, however, which is familiar to *Dasein* includes the ontological condition that makes it possible for *Dasein's* understanding to bring to light meaning and signification. These, in turn, form the basis of words and language.[30] We will return to the question of language in Chapter Ten.

Concluding we may thus say that, under the heading of the worldhood of the world, Heidegger investigates

[29] *S.Z.,* p. 87.
[30] *S.Z.,* p. 87.

the world of *Dasein* in its everydayness in contrast to the derivative world of science. It has its center in *Dasein* itself and originally it coincides with our own environment (*Umwelt*) insofar as this environment is experienced in our lived experiences. Heidegger show impressively how the things within this world are given *not* as physical objects which simply occur as obviously present-at-hand (*vorhanden*), but as usable things or pieces of equipment (*Zeuge*) which refer to possible applications within our "practical" world and are thus "ready-to-hand" or "handy" (*zuhanden*). Things of this type refer to one another and constitute reference-systems and only within these systems does the meaning of these things become manifest.

Heidegger's investigation of things in their surroundings shows how closely things are related to the world, and how closely both are connected with man as *Dasein*. He also shows that the world is not a thing, nor the sum of things, but rather the *a priori* totality toward which the different pieces of equipment point by their structures, their "for . . . what's" (*Um-zu*). What we call "world," taken in the strictest and most original sense, is *the totality of all mutual reference-systems within which every thing is to be put by man as* Dasein *in order to be able to appear to man as having such or such de-determinate meaning.* Dasein first builds up this world by means of its concern (within the context of a historical society), and then lives and dwells in it.

CHAPTER FOUR

SPATIALITY AND SPACE

In the explanation of the "being in" proper to *Dasein* as being-in-the-world, it was pointed out that this "being in" should not be understood in a spatial sense. Yet *Dasein* does possess a certain spatiality, and this will now be our topic. After an introductory consideration of the spatiality of intraworldly be-ings, we will pay special attention to the spatiality of *Dasein* itself and its relation to "space."[1]

1. THE SPATIALITY OF INTRAWORDLY BE-INGS

Closeness

If space somehow belongs to the world, then intraworldly be-ings must have spatiality. This point was already implicitly affirmed in our analysis of the onto-logical structure of intraworldly be-ings. Among the things which are "ready to hand" there are some which are proximally "ready to hand"; indeed, the concept of "closeness" is implied in the expression "ready to hand." This closeness is, of course, different in each concrete case and, as should be clear from the foregoing, this closeness cannot be measured by yardsticks taken from "pure" space.

The closeness of equipment is regulated by the use we make of it. Things which we frequently use are closer to us than others which we rarely need. *Dasein* in its concernful dealing with things gives each its place ac-cording to the importance it has in life. Each piece of equipment has its place within the totality of the equip-mental context of our everyday concern. Thus the close-ness of equipment is primordially defined by an organiza-

[1] *S.Z.*, p. 102.

tion whose ordering principle lies in *Dasein's* activities.

The space which arises in this way has no relation to geometric space, of which we will speak later. The various places of space, in the sense we take it here, do not all have the same importance; their hierarchy is determined by the degree of necessity which the pieces of equipment have for the work that has to be done.

"Place," therefore, means here the location which *Dasein* gives to a piece of equipment within a certain equipmental complex in function of its destination with regard to the work to be done. The various places in a certain space are thus related in the same manner as pieces of equipment within a certain equipmental complex.[2]

Region

Before *Dasein* can assign places, a region (*Gegend*) has to be discovered in which they will appear in the intended connection. Usually such a region is said to be the sum of places; it appears, however, that the region is rather the necessary condition for the assignment of places. One should also keep in mind that a place is never an isolated point sufficient unto itself, but a place necessarily means a relation to other places. Being remote from one another, orientation, and position in reference to one another always presuppose the region.

Place

The given hierarchy of places within a certain region determines the typical character of *Dasein's* world, which Heidegger calls "aroundness" (*das Umhafte*). As we have mentioned, the hierarchy of places itself is dependent on the function and destination of each piece of equipment that has its place in the hierarchy. Hence the places cannot be deduced from pure distance since the latter excludes all forms of hierarchy and does not consider the worldly character of space. Thus it follows that space

---

[2]*S.Z.,* pp. 102-103.

cannot be understood separately and independently from the be-ings that occupy it. On the contrary, space gets its meaning from these be-ings. *Dasein* does not first discover space itself, but rather the places; that is, in our everyday concern with intraworldly things, space is given in the form of places which the different pieces of equipment occupy within a certain equipmental totality.

Dasein discovers the places of the things that are "merely there" but assigns them to the things that are "ready to hand." In this way I discover the place of the sun in the sky, but I assign a place to my pen within the equipmental totality needed for writing. *Dasein* meets the region only in its action; the discovery of this region, however, is connected with the discovery of the referential context in which each piece of equipment becomes meaningful to *Dasein*.

As in the case of the "ready to hand," *Dasein* in its everyday concern is familiar with the region, the work domain, without grasping it explicitly and as such. Only the deficient modes of concernfulness make the region explicitly conscious to *Dasein;* for example, only when a piece of equipment appears not to be present, does *Dasein* become conscious of its place as place.[3]

2. Dasein's Spatiality

Dasein Spatializes

People usually say that first there is empty space and that this space is subsequently filled in some way. According to Heidegger, however, worldhood is the basis for the referential relations between pieces of equipment and these relations in turn are the foundation for the various places. In all this *Dasein* exercises a spatializing function. Since we have defined the spatiality of what is "ready to hand" in terms of the place which it occupies, the question arises of how we are to describe *Dasein's* spatiality.

[3] *S.Z.,* pp. 103-104.

Would there not be the same difference between these two forms of spatiality as between the modes of being proper to the two be-ings to which they belong? *Dasein's* being in space, at any rate, must be conceived in terms of the relations which unite *Dasein* with its familiar "ready to hand" things. The spatiality of its "being in" is determined by the activities of "removing distance" (*Ent-fernung*), i.e., "bringing close," and of "giving directions" (*Ausrichtung*), i.e., "situating."

Dasein "Brings Close"

First of all, *Dasein* makes distance and farness disappear. We may even say that *Dasein* essentially removes distances: it brings be-ings close so that they become "ready to hand." In doing so, *Dasein* implicitly discovers distances, for distance appears to *Dasein* only insofar as *Dasein* "brings close." A point is not away from another point, for a point cannot bridge the distance, it cannot make it larger or smaller, it does not 'bring close." Distances manifest themselves only to *Dasein's* activities of "bringing close." In everyday life this "bringing close" is always a question of circumspective, concernful dealing with things. By bringing be-ings close, *Dasein* wants to make these things available to itself and keep them so. In a derivative sense the different forms of theoretical knowledge also have something of this "bringing close."

Accordingly, in *Dasein* there is an essential tendency to closeness; speed records, radio, television and space travel can be viewed in this perspective. But this "bringing close" itself does not yet give *Dasein* explicit awareness of space. In everyday life, remoteness is never understood as sheer distance; all judgments of concernful *Dasein* refer to its concernful dealing with intraworldly be-ings and are more interested in "lived" estimates, such as "a stone's throw," than in the exact measurements of the sciences. Even when *Dasein* uses scientific measurements and views, it understands them only in terms of its everyday concernful dealing with things. For example, one hour is for *Dasein* primordially not a duration of sixty minutes but the time needed to perform this or that work.

If the estimate of *Dasein* does not coincide with that of science, it should not be said to be therefore wrong or subjective. If, for example, the distance of three miles is ten times as long for a sick person as for a healthy one, the sufferer is not necessarily mistaken, for he needs indeed ten times as much energy as the healthy person to go that distance. This "subjectivity" has nothing to do with arbitrariness; it is nonsense to oppose to *Dasein's* world a "world in itself" as the only real world. The world which *Dasein* discovers in its concernful dealing with things is the real world: *"Dasein's* circumspective 'bringing together' in its everyday concern discovers the 'true world,' the be-ings near which *Dasein,* as existing, is already."[4]

The spatiality of *Dasein,* which is essentially being-in-the-world, is not to be compared with scientific space; the distances of concernful living cannot be compared with objective measurements but are defined only by that activity of *Dasein* in which it concernfully deals with things and by the directing intention that created them. *Dasein's* "bringing close" does not consist in placing a thing closer to the "body," but in placing it within the sphere of things that are "ready to hand," that is, by making this thing itself "ready to hand." The "bringing closer" is not oriented toward our "body" but toward the center of our everyday concern. It is even false to state that our "body" occupies a place similiar to the places of "material bodies." The place of our "body" also should be understood only in terms of these activities of "bringing close."[5]

When *Dasein* speaks of "here" it does not mean a point of space, but only the "whereat" of its present occupation. *Dasein* is not a being closed in itself; it is always already

4*S.Z.*, p. 106.
5*S.Z.*, p. 107.

"there" (*Da*), near a piece of equipment or near a piece of work to be done. Its "here" is only the center of all "theres." For this reason *Dasein* never moves according to the demands of geometry from one point to another, it can only change its "here." Likewise, *Dasein* cannot cross over certain distances, for these distances are not fixed but precisely projected from the place where *Dasein* is concernfully active. *Dasein* cannot eliminate distances either, it can do no more than change them.[6]

Dasein "Situates"

As being-in-the-world *Dasein* "brings close" and at the same time "situates." It has a character of "directionality."[7] Whenever *Dasein* "brings close," a certain situating is implied within a region. This situating brings to light directions and regions which *Dasein* can subsequently use. By its existence *Dasein* brings close and situates regions, and in doing this it is led by its circumspection. Fundamentally both bringing close and situating are based on *Dasein's* being-in-the-world itself.[8]

Existential Character of Dasein's Spatializing Activity

In our consideration of the world we came to the conclusion that *Dasein* as being-in-the-world already has discovered a "world." This discovery frees be-ings within a certain referential context: *Dasein* lets be-ings be (*Bewendenlassen*) by discovering them within a certain referential context for a totality of destinations. *Dasein* is guided in this by circumspection, which in turn presupposes knowledge of significance as worldhood of the world. We had seen also that be-ings are not attained in their spatiality unless *Dasein* itself spatializes. By establishing a context of references *Dasein* discovers spatiality, that is, the place of a piece of equipment within the referential context and

---

[6]*S.Z.*, pp. 107-108.
[7]*S.Z.*, p. 108.
[8]*S.Z.*, pp. 108-110.

through this context within the region in which this context is situated. What is "ready to hand" is not first a-spatial but already has a place which by virtue of its own destination is determined for it.

There is no question yet of geometric space here, but only of the place which belongs to a piece of equipment within an equipmental totality. *Dasein* gives itself and the equipment a place, it assigns the places, makes room for what is "ready to hand," discovers the place proper to each be-ing, even though a spatial determination is always proper to the totality of characteristics of the intraworldly be-ing.[9] *Dasein's* spatializing activity is an existentiale. Because of this fundamental characteristic, *Dasein* can install itself in space, it can assign a place to be-ings and, when necessary, also change this place again.

A Priori of Space

In Heidegger's view, therefore, space is not in the subject, nor is the world in space. But, one may ask, is it possible to conceive space as being neither subjective (Kant) nor objective (Democritus)? Heidegger says that there appears to be a third possibility: "Space is rather 'in' the world insofar as space has been discovered by the being-in-the-world which is constitutive for *Dasein*."[10] Space is neither subjective nor objective, but *Dasein* spatializes. Because *Dasein* is neither a pure *ego* nor a pure subject, traditional subjectivism is radically transcended. Since, however, *Dasein* itself spatializes, space is an *a priori* element, in the sense that *Dasein's* nature founds the discovery of space, a discovery which is only possible in *Dasein's* encounter with be-ings.

Science and Space

Generally spatiality is never conceived as such, but remains attached to what is "ready to hand" and therefore

---

[9]*S.Z.*, p. 111.
[10]*S.Z.*, p. 111.

to *Dasein's* concernful dealing with things. Space discovers itself primordially only to concernful *Dasein* and remains as such connected with the spatiality, i.e., the places, of pieces of equipment. But because of this discovery, because of this presence of spatiality, *Dasein* can develop a theoretical science of pure space.

Heidegger does not claim that these replies fully solve the problem of space, but he only wants to throw light on the function of space in the structure of *Dasein's* daily concern. He appears to approach the problem in the right way because space is primordially present in our everyday life; and only by starting from this primordial presence can we obtain knowledge of space as such. The preceding analyses make us understand how space is primordially encountered, but the fundamental problem of the ontological value of space remains still unsolved.

The sciences certainly are not able to solve this problem, for scientific space abstracts from every relationship of space to the world. The places which have their own role and their own character in the world are stripped of all individuality in the eye of the sciences. In this way spatiality loses its character of destination. In the sciences the world in which *Dasein* concernfully lives changes into a scientific world, into "nature" as a correlate of the positive sciences, and what is "ready to hand" is ultimately reduced to an extended being that is "merely there." Thus the homogeneous and isotropic space of science deprives what is "ready to hand" of its worldhood.

In our era, however, we are so strongly influenced by the sciences that we find *Dasein's* primordial attitude toward space difficult to understand. Heidegger's main intention is to try to make us understand this primordial attitude.[11]

---

[11]*S.Z.*, pp. 110-113.

CHAPTER FIVE

BEING-IN-THE-WORLD AS "BEING WITH"

The preceding chapters have merely offered a preliminary idea of being-in-the-world. In the analyses of the world's worldhood and spatiality, the whole phenomenon of being-in-the-world was always included in our considerations; but the constitutive structure of being-in-the-world did not stand out as distinctively as the phenomenon "world" itself. The ontological interpretation of the world came first because *Dasein* in its everyday life is not only in the world but also related to it in a very special way. For this reason it was necessary to devote a few considerations to spatiality and space. Now, however, we must pay attention to the other constitutive structures of being-in-the-world. Two of these structures are indicated by "being with" (*Mitsein*) and "*Dasein* with others" (*Mitdasein*), which are just as primordial as being-in-the-world itself. Only after considering these structures will it be possible to answer the question "who" the *Dasein* is of everyday, concernful living.[1]

1. "BEING WITH" AND "DASEIN WITH OTHERS"

"Being With"

Concerning "being with," others are as equiprimordially present to *Dasein* as equipment is: in our dealing with intraworldly be-ings the presence of others is discovered at the same time because they also are involved in these pieces of equipment. A house belongs to someone, it is inhabited by someone and built by someone. It is therefore absurd to think that *Dasein* first encounters equipment and only afterwards, by abstraction and reflection, the others. We did not mention the others explicitly in the preceding analyses, but they were always implicitly

---

[1]*S.Z.*, pp. 113-114.

present; for the world cannot possibly be understood without any relation to them. As being-in-the-world, our existence is already a being together with others.

What exactly is this "being with" and what does it make fundamentally possible? At first one would be inclined to interpret "being with" as the co-presence of two simply given be-ings, in the sense in which even two marbles in a bag suffice to constitute a co-presence. What makes "being with" possible, however, is not the spatial proximity of two be-ings but their mutual relation. Where no mutual relation is possible there can be no "being with." In other words, "being with" is proper to *Dasein*.

The term "with" indicates a community: if I want to be "with" someone, there must be a certain communion between him and me. What we have in common binds us together. Sometimes even community is conceived as if it had a spatial aspect; so that whoever is closest is then "with" me. This is, of course, a false idea because it transfers a way of looking at things to *Dasein*. Things that are together often do constitute a unity, but this unity has nothing to do with a community. Genuine community has nothing to do with space; for example, travelers in the same train are often strangers to one another, while a friend away in Africa can be very close to me.

Another view of "being with" regards a common nature as the basis of being together. This could perhaps be defended, but one would have to be able to indicate clearly what is to be understood by "nature." To bring to light the different characteristics of "being with," it is probably best to start from concrete examples. Before doing so, however, it will be necessary to devote our attention to Sartre's critique of Heidegger's approach.

Sartre's Critique of Heidegger's Approach

Sartre has serious objections to Heidegger's way of thinking[2] and his critique appears to be very useful for a

---

[2]*L'Etre et le Néant,* p. 301.

correct understanding of Heidegger's intention.[3] According to Sartre, one should never pass from the ontological to the ontic level in considering topics such as these; therefore, one can never confirm a general theory with concrete examples.

However, Sartre's objection arises from the fact that he misunderstands the meaning which Heidegger attaches to the terms "ontological" and "ontic." The ontological level is not distinct from the ontic level, but precisely is the level which contains the essential structure of the ontic, which Sartre wrongly identifies with the concrete. Heidegger himself never speaks of the concrete since this immediately makes one think of the abstract; the antithesis between the concrete and the abstract is both meaningless and wrong here. There is no antithesis whatsoever between the ontological and the ontic. In this sense Heidegger says that *"Dasein* is ontically distinctive in that it *is* ontological."[4]

Such a statement becomes meaningless if one separates the ontic from the ontological as the concrete from the abstract and the immanent from the transcendent. For Heidegger, that which makes the being of things and of *Dasein* intelligible is ontological. In an ontological understanding of a be-ing one tries to grasp the essential structure which makes this be-ing possible as such. As long as this understanding is not yet explicit, it is called pre-ontological; properly ontological understanding is found in ontology, which raises the question of the meaning of being in a radical way. Hence the ontological belongs essentially to the ontic.[5]

In the ontological examination of the existentiel, one tries to make manifest that which is characteristic of ontic existence. The fundamental structures of *Dasein* are not abstract structures constituted by men, but real structures

---

[3]Cf. W. Biemel, *Le concept du monde chez Heidegger,* Louvain, 1950, pp. 67-74.
[4]*S.Z.,* p. 12.
[5]*S.Z.,* p. 13.

present in each concrete *Dasein*. Heidegger always starts from the ontic; ontology only explicitates what is included in the ontic as in the root which makes ontology possible. Sartre, however, separates them, so that his antithesis between the concrete and the abstract remains locked up within traditional metaphysics.

Secondly, Sartre thinks that the difference on this point between Hegel and Husserl, on the one hand, and Heidegger, on the other, lies in this that for the former "being with" expresses an opposition while for the latter it means primarily a solidarity.[6] This is incorrect, in the sense that Heidegger does not yet want to speak about the various types of man's "being with" but only about the conditions which make possible love as well as hatred, solidarity as well as indifference. Every relationship with others presupposes already "being with." For Heidegger, "being with" does not necessarily mean to live in harmony, but only that man from the first moment of his existence lives in a certain openness in which the other is already enclosed. Only because of this fundamental openness to the other are the different types of "being with" possible.

Concrete Example of "Being With"

But let us try to understand "being with" concretely through an example taken from daily life. When two people admire a painting and are similarly affected by it, this harmony of feelings brings them closer together, it develops a bond between them which could become the root of a community. What exactly occurred there? Together, the one with the other, they looked at a painting. The one entered the domain which was being unveiled by the other; the be-ing which became manifest in it to the one also became manifest to the other. Thus the one shared with the other that which had become open to him in his world and thereby shared that world itself with the other.

---

[6] *L'Etre et le Néant,* p. 303.

This sharing in one world is what constitutes their being together. Because of the fact that they share in one world they have something in common, viz., this world. On the basis of this common possession of one world, a community can be constituted according to the different modalities of "being with," which range from love to hatred, from solidarity to indifference.

"Dasein With Others" in a Common World

As we have pointed out above, what is "ready to hand" in everyday life always refers to an other as to its maker or its user. For this reason there is never any completely isolated *Dasein*. As soon as *Dasein* discovers the world, it has also already discovered the other who co-exists with him, who is also in the same way open to other be-ings and who, therefore, insofar as he shares in the same world, enters into a mutual relation with *Dasein*.

"Thus *Dasein's* world frees be-ings which not only are quite different from equipment and things, but which also, in accordance with their mode of being as *Daseins,* themselves are 'in' the world as 'being-in-the-world' and are at the same time encountered in an intraworldly way. These be-ings are neither 'merely there' nor 'ready to hand'; on the contrary, they are like the *Dasein* itself which frees them: they are there 'too,' and are there 'with' it."[7] "By reason of this 'with'-like (*mithaften*) being-in-the-world, the world is always the one that I share with others. The world of *Dasein* is our world, a 'with-world' (*Mitwelt*). 'Being in' is 'being with' others. Their intraworldly being 'in itself' is '*Dasein* with others' (*Mitdasein*)."[8] Heidegger refers here to "being with" others by means of two different words, *Mitsein,* i.e., my being with others, and *Mitdasein,* i.e., the being "open" (*da*) of the other to me and other people. Seen from my standpoint the other's way of

---

[7] *S.Z.*, p. 118.
[8] *S.Z.*, p. 118.

being is *"Dasein* with" me and others. I can discover the others as co-existent because I myself am "being with," that is, I share with them my openness to things and the world.

Although "being with," then, presupposes an equality of nature, co-existence is possible only because this equality of nature applies to be-ings which by their nature are open to whatever manifests itself to them and which therefore can share the world that is common to them.

The Mistake of Modern Philosophy

The basic mistake of modern philosophy since Descartes lies, according to Heidegger, in the fact that it understands the human "subject" too narrowly. Modern philosophy starts with a pure subject to whom it later tries to give a world, and still later it tries to bring this subject in contact with others. Such post-surgical constructions of the world and of man's fellow subjects are arbitrary and meaningless. Preoccupied lest it presuppose anything whatsoever regarding the subject's essence, modern philosophy fails to comprehend *Dasein* in its complexity, that is, as a be-ing which is already being-in-the-world, which is open to other things and other *Daseins* and which coexists with them. Heidegger intends to avoid this fundamental mistake. For this reason he does not divorce man from the world or conceive the world as a sum of things, but starts from being-in-the-world and attempts to attain from there a more profound vision of the world.

"Solicitude" and "Attention"

Heidegger characterizes the way men act toward one another as "solicitude" (*Fürsorge*). Solicitude, too, indicates an existentiale and encompasses *all* modalities of men's behavior toward one another. Thus it includes much more than what is usually conveyed by the term "solicitude." To neglect someone, to be against someone, and to hate someone—these are possible forms of solicitude.

As we have seen, *Dasein* is related to what is "ready to hand" through its everyday "concern," and this concern's own vision of things is called "circumspection." With respect to other *Daseins,* Heidegger speaks of "solicitude" (*Fürsorge*) and "attention" (*Rücksicht*). This last term has to be taken in a very broad sense so that it can also indicate the more negative modes of "regard."

No Isolated Subjects

"Being with" discloses the existence of others to us. This disclosing of the others' existence is also a co-constitutive element of "significance" (*Bedeutsamkeit*) : "The others' disclosedness, constituted beforehand with their 'being with,' also goes to make up significance, that is, worldhood."[9] For this reason we cannot first isolate a world of things in order to add a world of subjects to it later; the existence of others is co-present with the equipment encountered in our everyday concern. The world's structure of worldhood is such that others are not present in it as "free-floating subjects" next to other intraworldly be-ings, but manifest themselves in the world in their own being and do so in terms of what is "ready to hand" in the world. *Dasein* is primordially with the others; it is therefore nonsense to make the others' constitution dependent upon empathy as Scheler and Husserl have done.

One could object that Heidegger's view of "being with" leaves no more room for the phenomenon of "being alone." His reply is that "being alone" is essentially a separation of oneself from the others and therefore is not possible without a certain understanding of the other. Separation and isolation presuppose the existence of others so that "being alone" is possible only on the basis of a previous "being with."[10]

[9]*S.Z.,* p. 123.
[10]*S.Z.,* p. 121.

2. THE "WHO" OF DASEIN IN ITS EVERYDAY CONCERN

After these remarks about "being with" we must now try to find an answer to our initial question: Who is *Dasein* in its everyday concern? The answer seems very simple: I myself, of course. Selfhood is essential to *Dasein*. But what precisely is that "I myself"? What is this selfhood? In ordinary speech "self" refers to a real be-ing which, despite the many changes it undergoes, continues to remain itself. However, we have repeatedly emphasized that *Dasein* is not a thing among things and that its being is not even given once and for all. *Dasein* also lacks permanent characteristics such as those ascribed to things that are "merely there." How then is selfhood to be understood? Moreover, one has also to keep in mind that the words "in its everyday concern" are deliberately part of the question. Is it not possible that the "I myself" which I would like to be is not the "I myself" which I am in everyday life? Can the "I" not lose itself and is the "I" of everyday life not always an "I" that has already lost itself?[11]

The Impersonal "They"

In our consideration of "being with" it became evident that *Dasein* in its everyday concern is radically and inexorably dependent on the others.[12] If I ask myself to whom I am really subject and upon whom I am precisely dependent, this question cannot be answered. In everyday life my existence seems to be necessarily heteronomous without my being able to concretely indicate who determines this heteronomy. In the morning I have to be at the station on time; I have to be in school or at work on time; I have to sleep during the night and work during the day if I want to succeed with my business. Of course, I can withdraw from these "obligations," but this withdrawal merely binds me immediately with other fetters

[11]*S.Z.*, pp. 114-115.
[12]*S.Z.*, p. 126.

inherent to these other possibilities of my being which I then want to realize. The unnameable tyrant upon whom I am inescapably dependent is a neutral and impersonal subject; this is the "they" (*das Man*). In my everyday life I have to bow to the dictatorship of the impersonal "they." This "they" is the "subject" of my everyday existence, which at all moments and on all occasions of my life dictates what I should do and should be. In my everyday life the "I" is fully submerged in the "they."

The Dictatorship of the "They"

The "they" cultivates averageness as the norm of everything. It has only one yardstick, which is used for everyone and everything on every conceivable occasion. This averageness must always and anywhere be respected. If anyone deviates from this norm, he is condemned and called to order with all possible means. Total levelling down, even in the smallest details, is its ideal. No one is allowed to keep personal secrets, for everyone has to be open to everyone and merge with all others. Because the "they" does not tolerate any critique of its authority in any matter, the personal sense of responsibility is taken away from everybody. Whatever decision I face, the "they" have long ago prescribed what should be done in such a case. Since the "they" is responsible for everything, no one has really any responsibility at all. Under this yoke of bondage it is not possible any longer to be oneself; in exchange for this, the "they" gives security, tranquillity and guarantee. Under the dictatorship of the "they" everyone is someone else and no one is himself. The "they" is actually the "nobody" to whom every *Dasein* has already surrendered itself in everyday life.[13]

The "They" is an Existentiale

As long as one lives in this way, the self of one's own *Dasein* and the selves of others have not yet found or lost

[13]*S.Z.*, p. 128.

themselves. They are here in the way of inauthenticity and failure to stand by themselves.

These remarks, however, should not be misunderstood. What has been said here about the "they" has a very real sense. "This way of being does not imply any lessening of *Dasein's* facticity, just as the 'they,' the 'nobody,' is by no means nothing at all. On the contrary, in this kind of being, *Dasein* is an *ens realissimum,* if by 'reality' we mean a be-ing having the character of *Dasein*."[14] Nor is it the intention here to reduce *Dasein* to a thing that is "merely there." The "they" is a mode of being proper to *Dasein,* even though this mode is precisely that in which *Dasein* is not itself. The "they" also has nothing to do with a kind of "general subject" or "collective subject" in the sense in which it is sometimes used in sociology. "The 'they' is an existentiale, and as a primordial phenomenon, it belongs to *Dasein's* positive constitution."[15] It is also important to note that these considerations of the "they" have no ethical character.[16]

The self of everyday *Dasein* is the "they-self." It must be carefully distinguished from man's authentic self. As "they-self," *Dasein* in its everyday concernful dealing with things is already "dispersed." This dispersal characterizes the "subject" that is concernfully absorbed and lost in the world of its immediate surroundings. If *Dasein* in its everyday life is familiar with itself as a "they-self," this means at the same time that the "they" essentially determines the first interpretation of the world and of being-in-the-world.

Everything therefore that has been discovered above about the world and intraworldly be-ings, as well as everything that thus became clear concerning *Dasein* and *"Dasein* with," presupposed that *Dasein* was taken in its primordial mode of being, namely, in the way of the "they-self."[17]

---

[14]*S.Z.,* p. 128.
[15]*S.Z.,* p. 129.
[16]*S.Z.,* pp. 175-176.
[17]*S.Z.,* p. 129.

CHAPTER SIX

"BEING IN" AS SUCH. THE FUNDAMENTAL STRUCTURE OF *DASEIN*

1. DASEIN'S OPENNESS

From the very start our existential analysis of *Dasein* has been guided by being-in-the-world. The purpose of the analysis was to bring to light through the phenomeno-logical method the unitary primordial structure of *Dasein's* being, in terms of which its possibilities, its modes of being, can be determined. Until now this analysis has placed emphasis on the structural aspect called "world" and at-tempted to answer the question of "who" *Dasein* is in everyday life. At the very beginning, we spoke in an introductory fashion about "being in."

We now want to examine the structural element of "being in" itself. The outcome of this examination will throw a completely new light on what has already been said. At the same time we hope to have an opportunity to emphasize again the unity of the structure of *Dasein's* being, for this unity could easily have been obscured by the necessity of making distinctions.[1] We should keep in mind that the different structural elements of *Dasein's* being are all irreducible and equiprimordial, although they were considered and clarified one by one.[2]

In our further explanation of the "being in" proper to being-in-the-world, we start from what we have already discovered regarding "being in." These discoveries were mainly expressed in negative statements. We must now try to describe "being in" in positive terms. In this posi-tive description emphasis will be put on the *Da* of *Dasein*, i.e., its openness to the world. As we have indicated above, this *Da* has nothing to do with a spatial here or there, for such spatial indications refer only to intraworldly

[1]*S.Z.*, pp. 130-131.
[2]*S.Z.*, p. 131.

be-ings. The spatial "here" and "there" are possible only through a *Da,* i.e., if there exists a be-ing that as *Dasein* has disclosed spatiality. *Dasein's* own being is character- ized by openness. "The particle *Da* refers to this essential openness. By reason of this openness, this be-ing (*Dasein*), together with the 'being there' of the world, is 'there' for itself."[3]

This existential-ontological structure of the human be-ing, namely, that it is in such a way as to be its own *Da* (=openness), can also be expressed by saying that man is a *lumen naturale,* a "natural light." *Dasein* itself is "enlightened"; as being-in-the-world, it is "lighted" in itself in such a way that it is itself a "place of light." Things that are "merely present" and themselves concealed in darkness can come to light only through a be-ing that is itself "lighted."

We must now ask ourselves how the *Da* of *Dasein,* its openness, is constituted. Here also we will discover con- stitutive elements which, although they form an unbreak- able unity, will have to be studied one by one. Heidegger expresses these elements in the following words: "We see the two equiprimordial constitutive modes of being *Da* in 'understanding' and 'moodness.' 'Moodness' and 'under- standing' are characterized equiprimordially by logos."[4] We must now see what is to be understood by these terms, "moodness" (*Befindlichkeit*),[5] "understanding" (*Verste- hen*), and "logos" (*Rede*).

2. "MOODNESS"

Mood, Not Sentiment

In this existential-ontological discussion, what is meant by "moodness" is ontically something very familiar, our

---

[3]*S.Z.,* p. 132.
[4]*S.Z.,* p. 133.
[5]"Befindlichkeit," the state in which one finds oneself, is some- times translated by "state of mind," "the sense of one's situation," and "the way in which one is 'placed' in life and in the world." (**Tr.**)

mood. No matter what we do, we always find ourselves in a certain mood. Heidegger carefully avoids the word "sentiment" because, according to him, this expression speaks in terms of an inacceptable opposition between "soul" and "spirit." Moreover, the use of the term "sentiment" easily conveys the impression that sentiments, and the soul connected with them, are regarded as merely secondary elements subordinated to the absoluteness of the spirit or reason (*ratio*). In this way one fails to pay attention to the great importance moods possess for correctly understanding man's own being. Besides, one usually omits explaining what is meant by spirit, soul and life, so that everything remains vague. Finally, such considerations divorce man as "subject" from the world.

It is likewise incorrect to consider sentiments as something purely "subjective" that would exist inside man and thus be opposed to the things outside him, which alone would be "objective." For, by doing that, one would again disregard the fundamental relationship between man and other be-ings.

Primordial Character of Mood

Accordingly, the terms "mood" and "affective disposition" should be taken to refer to that characteristic of *Dasein* whereby it always seems to be enlightened in one way or another about its own position among the things for which it is naturally open. Because of this basic mood, man realizes his own situation in the world: "Every way of acting of historical man, whether stressed or not, is 'tuned' to a mood and by this attunement raised to be-ing in its totality."[6] It cannot be denied that mood is something primordial which is characteristic of our being man.

What exactly is the ontological structure of this mood? This structure is very difficult to define because our thematic knowledge of affective life always appears to

[6]*Vom Wesen der Wahrheit,* p. 9.

be insufficient. Undoubtedly, the mood tells us something about our own being in its relation to other be-ings, but it is very difficult to indicate why one is in a certain mood and what this mood tells us about our own being: "*Dasein* cannot know anything of the sort because the possibilities of disclosure proper to cognition do not reach far enough compared with the primordial disclosure belonging to moods in which *Dasein* is brought before its being as '*Da.*' "[7]

Disclosure of "Thrownness"

Mood, then, discloses to man his situation among things. Several elements must be distinguished here. First, in his mood man is aware of his being, of the fact that he *is*. Without wanting it and without freely having chosen it, man *is*. His being appears to him as a "being thrown"; he appears to himself as thrown among be-ings. This Heidegger expresses with the term "thrownness" (*Geworfenheit*). In mood man not only becomes conscious of the fact "that he *is*," but also of the fact that he "has to be," that his being has to be realized by himself as a task.[8]

Disclosure of Being-in-the-World

Secondly, the fact that man is in this mood or in that mood depends upon the modalities of the involvement which he always has with things in the world. If one recognizes this it becomes evident that mood cannot be a phenomenon of secondary importance, but belongs to the most essential problems faced by the study of man's own being. Mood is an implicit, continuous "judgment" regarding our self-realization. Hence *Dasein* can be disclosed to itself in a more primordial way by mood than by theoretical reflection.

----

[7] *S.Z.*, p. 134.
[8] *S.Z.*, p. 135.

However, if *Dasein* is essentially being-in-the-world, then mood has to disclose to man not only his "being thrown," but also the world, other *Daseins* and things. "Having a mood is not directly related to the psychical, and is not itself an inner condition which then comes forth in an enigmatic way and puts its seal on things and persons. It is in this that the second essential characteristic of 'moodness' shows itself. 'Moodness' is a fundamental existential species of the equiprimordial disclosedness proper to the world, *'Dasein* with,' and existence, because this disclosedness itself is essentially being-in-the-world."[9]

Disclosure of the World's Worldhood

Thirdly, as we already said, *Dasein* in its everyday concern encounters intraworldly beings in terms of the horizon of the world taken as a referential totality. Thus the world has to be disclosed as such beforehand. Precisely because the world is given to *Dasein* beforehand, it is possible for *Dasein* to encounter intraworldly be-ings. This prior disclosedness of the world is co-constituted by one's mood. For example, an event can appear to us as terrifying only after *Dasein* finds itself in a mood of fear; the world can disclose the terrifying to man only because man is essentially defined by his "moodness," his being "attuned." In general, one can say that the many characteristics of the be-ings appearing within the world are as such made possible through the mood. This is what Heidegger wants to express in the following words: "The attunement of one's mood existentially constitutes *Dasein's* openness to the world."[10]

Sometimes the affection of the senses is explained by "pressure" exercised on organs endowed with sensibility. But no pressure whatsoever could stir our senses if we who undergo those pressures were not determined by the

---

[9] *S.Z.*, p. 137.
[10] *S.Z.*, p. 137.

mood through which we are open to things and through which precisely we can be affected by them: "Under the strongest pressure and resistance, nothing like an affect would come about . . . if being-in-the-world, with its 'moodness,' had not already submitted itself to having intra-worldly be-ings 'matter' to it in a way which its moods have outlined in advance. Existentially, 'moodness' implies a disclosing submission to the world, in terms of which one can encounter something that 'matters.' Onto-logically speaking, we must as a fundamental principle leave the primary discovery of the world to 'bare mood.' "[11]

3. PRIMORDIAL UNDERSTANDING

The second existentiale, the second essential structural aspect of *Dasein's* openness, is primordial understanding. *Dasein* not only possesses an existential possibility to be always in a mood, but it is equiprimordially understand-ing. Like the fundamental mood, this understanding is not a definition imposed on *Dasein* from without. It is not to be conceived as a mode of our knowing or explici-tating, but precisely as that which makes all modes of knowing possible. This primordial understanding is always already present in mood, and all understanding in its turn is connected with a particular mood. To *Dasein,* as being-in-the-world, its own being and the world are already dis-closed to some extent, and this being-disclosed is funda-mentally a kind of understanding. This understanding has to do with *Dasein's* own being, its fellow be-ings, and with things, but in such a way that any one of these three modes always somehow implies the other two.

Existential Possibilities

According to Heidegger, the term *Verstehen* (to under-stand) can be connected with *Vor-stehen,* in the sense of *prae-stare,* "to stand before" a thing in order to master it.

[11]*S.Z.,* pp. 137-138.

To be able to master something is a form of being able to be, a power to be. In primordial understanding this power to be is not a limited power but the essential possibility of being able to exist: *"Dasein* is not something 'merely there' which possesses a superadded power for something, but is primarily 'being able to be.' "[12] *Dasein* is what it can be, it is its possibilities.

In this connection it is important to distinguish clearly between existential and logical possibilities. The logical possibility indicates that what is not yet can be; this being-possible is less important than being-actual and being-necessary. The existential possibility, on the other hand, is the most primordial and the ultimate positive ontological characterization of *Dasein.*[13] This fundamental possibility has to do with the different modalities of concernful dealing with things and of solicitude while, at the same time, it constitutes the realization of *Dasein* itself.

That *Dasein* essentially is a power to be does not mean that *Dasein* is not actual, but only that, as it actually exists, it is certain possibilities and consequently excludes others. By choosing this particular possibility, *Dasein* has to abandon others. In this sense *Dasein* is essentially a power to be. This power is given to *Dasein* with its being. *Dasein* is thrown into the power to be, it is "thrown possibility through and through."[14] Through primordial understanding these possibilities become clear to *Dasein* so that it can take them up and realize them.

Project

The primordial understanding as the constitutive disclosure of *Dasein's* power to be also brings to light the world as referential totality. By disclosing the world to *Dasein,* primordial understanding also gives it the possibility to encounter intraworldly be-ings in their own possibilities. What is "present at hand" is discovered as a

---

[12]*S.Z.,* p. 143.
[13]*S.Z.,* pp. 143-144.
[14]*S.Z.,* p. 144.

be-ing which *can* serve to . . . , or which previously *could* serve to . . . but *can* no longer be used. The referential totality of equipment itself appears to us as a possible unity of be-ings; thus "nature" itself is always discovered in terms of a certain possibility.

Accordingly, primordial understanding always moves in the range of possibilities; it endeavors to discover possibilities. Heidegger indicates this characteristic of understanding by stating that understanding is a "project" (*Entwurf*). In its primordial understanding *Dasein* projects itself to an ultimate "what . . . for," but at the same time it projects itself also to a certain significance (*Bedeutsamkeit*), to a certain worldly structure. In this way the project gives *Dasein* the leeway of its power to be.[15] *Dasein,* then, is thrown into a mode of being which is ultimately determined by a project. By projecting itself, *Dasein* is its possibilities and therefore is what it becomes.

A Thrown Project

Later we will return to the temporal aspect of the project. Presently we only want to indicate that in his later works Heidegger tries to explain the project in terms of Being. In the "ec-static" project, he argues, Being discloses itself to *Dasein*. However, the project itself does not create Being. On the contrary, the project is essentially a thrown project and that which "throws" it is not man but Being. Being itself guides man in the existence of *Dasein* as in its essence.[16]

The French existentialists see the project as a completely free choice. Heidegger's *Being and Time* lends itself to a similar interpretation, but the same cannot be said of his later works. In the perspective of these works the fundamental choice of *Dasein* is not absolutely free; it is always limited by the openness achieved in existence which is the work of Being as such, executed by man.

---

[15]*S.Z.*, p. 145.
[16]*Brief über dem Humanismus,* p. 84.

Vision

According to *Being and Time,* man opens himself to the world and to his own being through primordial understanding; every mode of primordial understanding involves *Dasein* as being-in-the-world in its totality. For this reason primordial understanding implies essentially a certain view, a "sight," of things, of fellow be-ings and of *Dasein* itself. "In its character as a project, understanding makes up existentially what we call *Dasein's* 'sight' (*Sicht*)."[17] Heidegger wants to say here that being is disclosed through primordial understanding in what it is and as it is. This "sight" or view therefore has nothing to do with the functioning of any of the senses as such. The specific view ("sight") of *Dasein* which constitutes *Dasein* as such is circumspection (*Umsicht*), attention (*Rücksicht*) or transparency (*Durchsichtigkeit*), according to *Dasein's* fundamental ways of being, i.e., insofar as *Dasein's* view is concerned with equipment, fellow be-ings or *Dasein* itself. If *Dasein* knows itself from something that is not its authentic being, then this knowledge is inauthentic. This happens mainly when *Dasein* knows itself from its concernful dealing with equipment. Strictly speaking, *Dasein* knows itself only in its relation to Being. It is this knowledge which Heidegger wants to explicitate; for this reason it is necessary first to eliminate the inauthentic knowledge which is very widespread, even in traditional philosophy.

The existentialia of both "moodness" and primordial understanding are equiprimordial. They are also always found together. Without them, *Dasein* is not and cannot be understood. Primordial understanding is always marked by a mood, and a mood is also always a bringing to light. In its primordial understanding marked by a mood, *Dasein* must always of necessity choose one of the three modalities of knowing named above, viz., circomspection, attention or transparency.

---

[17]*S.Z.,* p. 146.

Understanding and Interpretation

Thus primordial understanding always has the character of an interpretative conception in which *Dasein* discloses itself as power to be in the different modalities that are possible here. In this sense primordial understanding is the constituting rather than the passive grasping of what is given. This interpretation, however, is as such not yet explicit in the understanding itself, but the various aspects of understanding come to clarity in its development and interpretation. *Dasein* discovers the meaning of things in the world through interpretation, which in the first instance is not yet a conceptional and discursive interpretation. Meaning is not a quality of a thing, but it is everything that a be-ing is and means to *Dasein*. An intraworldly be-ing therefore has meaning only in relation to *Dasein;* outside this relation it is not meaningless (*sinnlos*) but "unmeaningful" (*unsinnig*).

The primordial interpretation can also be explicitly formulated in an "assertion" (*Aussage*). The assertion does not necessarily, nor even primarily, have to be an expression in words; but it includes everything in which *Dasein* makes its primordial, previously interpreted understanding known, no matter in what way this is done. If this expression is made known through language, the reason is that discourse, like mood, always goes together with *Dasein's* primordial understanding. This brings us to the third constitutive element of *Dasein's* openness.

4. Logos

To survey what we have said so far about "moodness" and primordial understanding, we have to consider the aspect of *Dasein's* openness called "logos" or discursive reasoning (*Rede*). Logos was already implicitly present in the description of the two above-mentioned existentialia. By "logos" Heidegger means here *Dasein's* fundamental possibility to put in order and classify, to delimitate and structure. Without this possibility, "moodness" and primordial understanding are impossible, for " 'moodness' and understanding are characterized equiprimordially by logos."[18] Logos refers not only to intraworldly be-ings, the world and fellow be-ings, but especially to the proper being of *Dasein* itself.

Discursive reasoning or logos is the foundation of language, and originally language is nothing but logos become concrete. Since logos structures being-in-the-world, and since being-in-the-world is essentially coexistence, logos necessarily leads men to explain their viewpoints in common, which is precisely what language is. The function of the word, therefore, is not to make known externally what is within me. *Dasein* is not pure interiority or ipseity. As being-in-the-world, together with others, *Dasein* is essentially "outside itself" and this fundamental "eccentricity" is merely affirmed by the possibility of speech.

Language likewise does not bear witness to what we are in a secondary way; on the contrary, I am what I say, at least when there is question of primordial and authentic speech. There is also a form of speech which is inauthentic: it is the manner of speaking used by a *Dasein* that has become wholly absorbed in its concernful dealing with intraworldly things and thus has lost itself.

5. DASEIN'S "FALLENNESS"

We have already mentioned that, according to Heidegger, the being-in-the-world, which essentially characterizes *Dasein,* is a structure that can assume two different fundamental modalities, one authentic and the other inauthentic. We have also pointed out that what has been said above about the worldhood of the world and about "being in" describes that which immediately manifests itself to *Dasein* in its concernful dealing with intraworldly be-ings. In other words, we considered *Dasein* in its inauthenticity. In the preceding pages we have examined the fundamental structure of *Dasein's* openness, which is

---

[18]*S.Z.,* p. 133.

essential to *Dasein* in both ways of being. We now want to describe explicitly how the three existentialia of openness manifest themselves when *Dasein* has fallen into the inauthentic form of being.

The Constitutive Elements of Dasein's Inauthenticity

Heidegger likes to refer to the inauthentic being of *Dasein* as "fallenness" (*Verfallen*). Explaining this term, he says that it "does not express any negative evaluation, but is used to signify that *Dasein* is first of all and for the most part 'at' (*bei*) the 'world' of its concern. . . . *Dasein* has, in the first instance, fallen away from itself as an authentic power to be its own self, and has 'fallen' to the 'world.' "[19] The "world" is put in quotation marks to indicate that there is no reference here to the worldhood of the world, but only to what we encounter within our referential totality, namely the intraworldly be-ings with which we deal in our everyday concern and which the "they" usually identifies with the world.

"Fallenness" includes two aspects: 1. *Dasein* understands its own being in terms of intraworldly be-ings and thus conceives itself as a substance possessing certain qualities; 2. the world which is here present is the world of everyone, the world of the "they." The intraworldly be-ings, which are then considered to constitute the world, are only vaguely understood in the way the "they" generally understands them. The world in which *Dasein* is absorbed here is an impersonal world, just as its understanding of the world is also an impersonal form of understanding. " 'Fallenness' to the 'world' means to be absorbed in being with one another, insofar as this being is guided by idle talk, curiosity, and ambiguity."[20] Idle talk, curiosity and ambiguity are, for Heidegger, the three constitutive elements of *Dasein's* openness in its inauthentic being.

---

[19] *S.Z.*, p. 175. The German *bei* denotes more than mere proximity; the sense is closer to the "at" of "at home." (Tr.)
[20] *S.Z.*, p. 175.

Dasein lacks its primordial power to be in its inauthenticity and is likewise unable to realize its authentic self. "Fallenness" is not a form of not-being, but is ontically just as real as authentic existence. But *Dasein* here realizes itself in an inauthentic way so that it loses the typical way of being which it should strive to obtain. Each *Dasein* comes to authentic being only by way of inauthentic being and even thereafter there always is a real possibility that it will relapse into inauthenticity. *Dasein* then "falls" by losing its own way of being, it "falls" to the world as the total of intraworldly be-ings.

By identifying itself with this "world," its being becomes as impersonal as this "world" itself. In this "fall" it loses its authenticity, not its being as such; only its way of being becomes different. *"Dasein* plunges out of itself into·itself, into the groundlessness and nullity of inauthentic everydayness. But this plunge remains hidden from *Dasein* by the way things are publicly interpreted [by the 'they']—to such an extent that its fall is interpreted as a way of 'rising higher' and 'living concretely.' "[21]

Tranquillity and Restlessness

Dasein, then, is not aware of its fall, but regards it precisely as rising to a "concrete" form of life. Public opinion confirms it in this view and defends it against the restlessness which the great questions of life could possible arouse in it. The "they" has the answer ready before *Dasein* in its fallen condition gets a chance to become disturbed. The tranquillity (*Beruhigung*) which arises in this way is again one of the characteristics of *Dasein's* inauthenticity.[22]

Paradoxically, however, there is always a certain whirl and restlessness which dominate *Dasein*. *Dasein* wants to surrender itself to this restlessness because it does not really feel satisfied with the seeming tranquillity it possesses. It wants to have security, but it also wants to "live"; it

---

[21]*S.Z.*, p. 178
[22]*S.Z.*, p. 177.

wants to plunge into everything that presents itself in order to forget its emptiness. In spite of everything, it wants to realize itself and thinks to have found its authentic self in the illusion of an eternal restlessness. All this, however, is really but an attempt to deceive itself. It remains blind to its authentic being: "It has not been understood that understanding itself is a power to be which must be made free in one's *ownmost Dasein* alone."[23]

Alienation

By cultivating this restlessness, *Dasein* becomes more and more alienated from itself. This temptation to become more and more alienated from itself is also characteristic of *Dasein* in its inauthenticity. It feels attracted to empty and idle talk in which one chatters about everything without really saying anything, and to curiosity in which one gets interested in everything without ever really coming into contact with anything. In this way *Dasein* submerges increasingly more in an atmosphere of ambiguity and equivocity, in which ultimately, through all the talking and inquisitiveness, nobody knows any longer what actually is happening.[24]

Precisely this idle talk and curiosity usually bring about *Dasein's* "fallenness," by way of this atmosphere of ambiguity, because this is the road of the least resistance. Typical of "fallenness" is, however, that *Dasein* is tempted by the easy kind of being proper to the "they." This way of being is characterized, on the one hand, by tranquillity but, on the other, by the attractive alienation of the "whirl" (*Wirbel*), the plunge into inauthenticity.[25]

[23] *S.Z.*, p. 178.
[24] *S.Z.*, p. 174.
[25] *S.Z.*, p. 178.

CHAPTER SEVEN

DREAD AND CARE. TEMPORALITY AND TIME

Existential analytics endeavors to bring to light the structural elements of *Dasein's* own being and to consider them in detail. At the same time it must try to emphasize the fundamental unity of all these structural elements. Having attempted to describe these structural elements one by one, we must now consider how all these elements form a single whole, "the primordial totality of *Dasein's* whole structure."[1]

From the preceding chapters it is clear also that it is possible for *Dasein* to be in an inauthentic way as well as in an authentic way. Because so far we have only sketched *Dasein's* inauthentic being, we must now also face the questions of what precisely is meant by authentic being and how *Dasein* can come to be authentically. In the light of his previous analysis, Heidegger thinks that a thorough analysis of the phenomenon of dread can answer the second question, while a detailed study of care will be able to answer the first. Since we intend to return to the phenomenon of dread in one of the following chapters, we will confine ourselves here to what is required to answer these two questions.

1. DREAD

According to Heidegger, dread is a phenomenon which is *par excellence* suitable to throw light on the unity of *Dasein's* structural moments. "The entire phenomenon of dread (*Angst*) shows *Dasein* as actually existing being-in-the-world. The fundamental ontological characteristics of this be-ing are existentiality, facticity, and 'being

---

[1] *S.Z.,* p. 180.

fallen.' "[2] What Heidegger means by the terms existentiality, facticity, and "being fallen" has been sufficiently explained in the preceding chapters. Facticity is the technical term for the phenomenon of "being thrown"; and
existentiality indicates that *Dasein* projects itself, through
primordial understanding, to its own possibilities. This
self-projection is at the same time the discovery of be-ing.

Heidegger thinks that dread, which is "caused" by
these existentialia, places man before his primordial power
to be. For dread makes intraworldly be-ings disappear,
just as it also makes *Dasein's* fellow be-ings irrelevant.
"Dread . . . deprives *Dasein* of the possibility to understand itself, as it 'falls,' in terms of the 'world' and in the
way things are publicly interpreted [by the 'they']. Dread
throws *Dasein* back upon that which it dreads, viz., its
authentic power for being-in-the-world."[3] In dread *Dasein*
experiences the nothingness of its own being, realizes how
much it costs to exist and at the same time understands
the precariousness of this existence. Before we can clarify
these points, however, we must first say something about
care.

2. CARE

Dasein's Being "Ahead of Itself"

The fact that *Dasein* is essentially a power to be is
ontologically of extraordinary importance. As such a
power, *Dasein* is always "ahead of itself." This does not
mean that *Dasein,* as a power to be, necessarily implies a
relationship to those be-ings which it is not, but that
Dasein's being points to the power to be which it itself
is.[4] "*Dasein* is already *ahead* of itself in its being."[5]

---

[2]*S.Z.*, p. 191. The term *Angst* is variously translated as
"anxiety" and "dread." "Uneasiness" and "malaise" are other
suggested translations. (Tr.)
[3]*S.Z.*, p. 187.
[4]*S.Z.*, p. 192.
[5]*S.Z.*, p. 191.

Dasein is thus essentially defined by its power to be. In this sense it is always ahead of what it actually is and cannot even realize itself without previously anticipating this power to be. We have already met this anticipating feature when we spoke about primordial understanding, for this understanding proved to be essentially a project. Precisely because *Dasein* possesses the ontological structure of projecting, it can always be ahead of its actual being and will never cease to anticipate itself.

Being "Ahead of Itself" and Being-in-the-World

Every actual activity and every actual choice is made in reference to a certain power to be and is never more than a realization of a potentiality. This having to be "ahead of itself" can very appropriately be integrated in the total structure of *Dasein* as being-in-the-world. *Dasein* is always ahead of itself by being in a world and by being of necessity involved in it. This "being ahead," this project, constitutes what Heidegger calls "to ec-sist." In this sense, therefore, "to ec-sist" means that *Dasein* is ahead of itself according to its power to be. *Dasein* can realize its possibilities precisely because it is involved in the world. *Dasein* cannot go beyond itself without being "thrown" into the world. In other words, ec-sistence presupposes facticity. Existing is always factical. "Existentiality is essentially determined by facticity."[6]

Care as the Fundamental Structure of Dasein

Dasein, which in this way is in a world into which it is "thrown," always discovers itself there as absorbed in that which immediately manifests itself there and with which *Dasein* deals concernfully. Heidegger indicates this very concisely by saying that *Dasein's* being means "ahead-of-itself being-already-in (the world) as being 'at' (be-ings encountered within the world)."[7] *Dasein's*

[6] *S.Z.*, p. 192.
[7] *S.Z.*, p. 192.

having to be "ahead of itself," while at the same time taking into account the limits imposed by being thrown into the world, and while it really is always absorbed in the things of the world already, constitutes what Heidegger calls "care" (*Sorge*). Thus care is the necessary consequence of:

1) existentiality, that is, the fact that *Dasein* always has to transcend itself toward its power to be;

2) facticity, that is, being thrown;

3) and "being fallen," that is, the necessity of always having to be already "at" the things in the world.

Care, therefore, is the unity of these structural moments and has little connection with what is ordinarily called "care." It is not a condition of the mind but the fundamental structure of *Dasein* itself. Because *Dasein's* being is care (*Sorge*), its dealing with intraworldly beings is concern (*Besorgen*) and its relationship to its fellow be-ings is solicitude (*Fürsorge*).

In existing, i.e., being ahead of oneself toward one's power to be, lies the existential-ontological condition for *Dasein's* possibility of being free for its authentic, existential possibilities.[8] By transcending itself toward these possibilities, *Dasein* actually makes itself free for these possibilities. Existentiality therefore is also freedom. This primordial being free always contains ultimately the possibility of *Dasein's* authentic being.

Care, therefore, is not the resultant of various ways *Dasein* behaves toward other *Dasein's* or toward intraworldly be-ings, but refers to the fundamental structural unity which *a priori* makes all ways of *Dasein's* actual behaving possible: "As a primordial structural totality, care lies existentially *a priori* 'before' every factual 'attitude' and 'situation' of *Dasein,* that is, it always lies *in*

---

[8] *S.Z.,* p. 193.

them."[9] Heidegger expressly adds that this definition of *Dasein* is not intended to reduce *Dasein* by way of care to something which belongs solely to the perspective of practical pursuits. For care is precisely the basis not only of practical pursuits but also of any theory: " 'Theory' and 'practice' are possibilities of being for a be-ing whose being must be defined as 'care.' "[10]

3. TEMPORALITY

Care, however, does not suffice to reduce the constituent elements of *Dasein* to complete unity. Starting from care, one cannot go beyond a structural unity. We therefore must continue our analysis in order to bring to light the ultimate ontological foundation which constitutes this primordial unity. Heidegger finds this foundation in *Dasein's* temporality, to which he has devoted the second part of *Being and Time*. In this chapter we will not enter into all the problems raised by Heidegger in connection with temporality and time, but will limit ourselves to what is relevant to the matters considered here. Later we will have an opportunity to devote our attention to some of the other problems of temporality and time.

Dasein's Essentially Unfinished Character

Heidegger begins by asking whether *Dasein* can be understood as a whole since as being-in-the-world it is an existing be-ing.[11] In the light of what has been said before, this seems at first impossible. First of all, *Dasein* because of its existentiality is essentially "unsettled," unfinished. By virtue of its existentiality, *Dasein* has, in principle, always to transcend itself toward its own power to be, so that it is always and authentically "on the way." As long as *Dasein* has not yet attained the terminus of its being-in-the-world, it remains unfinished insofar as

---

[9] *S.Z.*, p. 193.
[10] *S.Z.*, p. 193.
[11] *S.Z.*, pp. 235-236.

there always remain possibilities which have to be realized; once, however, it has attained its terminus, it immediately stops existing. Secondly, one could, of course, try to understand being-in-the-world as a whole in terms of this terminus or death. But even this is not very well possible because death, as entrance into "nothingness," can never be experienced.

Upon closer examination, however, there seems to be a possible solution. *Dasein* is really always unfinished and even constitutionally unfinished, just as an unripe fruit is unfinished. Nevertheless, there is a major difference between *Dasein* and an unripe fruit. When the fruit is ripe it has attained its wholeness, while death takes man at a moment when there are still possibilities to be realized. Seen in this way, death cannot help explain the problem. However, it can also be considered in a different way, not only as the "point" where *Dasein's* life reaches its end, but also as that toward which *Dasein* is always "on the way." Taken in this last sense, death seems to offer a possibility to understand *Dasein* as being-in-the-world in its wholeness. We must now try to see how this is possible.[12]

Being Toward Death

Living in inauthenticity, "one" sees death as an inevitable fact which the entire human race has to face. Many die, but "one" sees that it is not one's turn yet. This way "one" escapes the dread of the reality of being toward death.[13] But the most essential point is not that death is an inevitable "fact," but that *Dasein* is a being toward death. "The 'end' we have in mind when we speak of death does not signify *Dasein's* 'being at an end,' but a 'being toward the end' of this be-ing. Death is a way to be, which Dasein takes over as soon as it is."[14]

[12]*S.Z.*, pp. 236-237.
[13]*S.Z.*, p. 254.
[14]*S.Z.*, p. 245.

Death, of course, is a possibility of man's being—the possibility that leads to *Dasein's* "being no more." Death is our ultimate possibility because our being-in-the-world itself is at stake here. Death reveals to me the "possibility of my further impossibility"; discovering death makes me understand the radical finiteness of my life. It is the fundamental possibility which from the beginning leaves its mark upon my life. "In fact, *Dasein* is dying as long as it exists."[15]

Since *Dasein* is being-in-the-world toward death, it is evident that *Dasein* is essentially dread. Thus it is also clear how in this view of death one has the possibility to understand *Dasein* in its wholeness. For, "in *Dasein,* as being toward its death, its own ultimate 'not yet' has already been included—that 'not yet' which all others lie ahead of"[16] in the sense that they may come about before *Dasein's* ultimate "not yet" has been realized. We also get a more correct view of authentic being in this manner. In authentic being one thinks death away, while in authentic being one dares to face death. Also, *Dasein* which has come to authentic being expects death; it knows that death is already constitutive for all its possibilities. Death reveals here the "nothing" as the ultimate possibility. Man sees himself placed alone before this "nothing" and he realizes from this, therefore, that all his projects are "nothing." Yet *Dasein* dares to keep on acting, though it understands the meaninglessness of action in the light of death and though it knows that it cannot expect help from anyone here.[17]

The Meaning of Care and Being Toward Death

In a later passage of *Being and Time* Heidegger returns explicitly to what is our main problem here: "When we ask about the meaning of care, we are asking, What makes

15 *S.Z.,* p. 251.
16 *S.Z.,* p. 259. The "not yet" is *Dasein's* power to be that which has not yet been realized. (Tr.)
17 *S.Z.,* pp. 265-266.

possible the totality of the articulated structural whole of care, in the unity of its articulation as it has been unfolded here?"[18] In order to find a solution of the problem, Heidegger first returns to what he has said about meaning (*Sinn*). Every understanding develops according to a certain dimension, and this dimension determines *a priori* the character of being of what will thus be understood. To understand the meaning of a be-ing does not mean to understand something outside this be-ing, but to discover the being itself of this be-ing. Heidegger speaks about meaning when one understands the being of a be-ing. Usually one does not understand explicitly the meaning of a be-ing. "Meaning is that in which the understandability of something maintains itself, without this 'something' itself coming into view explicitly and thematically. Meaning signifies the 'upon which' (*Woraufhin*) of the primary project in terms of which something can be understood in its possibility, as that which it is."[19]

This "upon which" indicates the perspective and dimension in which a thing appears to us. In each project concerning intraworldly be-ings, however, the world itself plays a role. The reason is that if a thing is to manifest itself as an intraworldly be-ing, *Dasein* has to follow up its fundamental project of the world; for only this project makes it possible for *Dasein* to encounter a be-ing as intraworldly.

Heidegger's "project" of the world has no connection whatsoever with an idealistic constitution of the world or with Husserl's "giving of meaning." Heidegger wants to refer only to a disclosure of the world which has to make it possible to encounter any be-ing. Man, however, cannot encounter anything outside his world because the world constitutes the foundation of every encounter; hence any discovery of meaning has to take place "within" the world. As soon as man opens himself toward the world, he can encounter be-ings.

---

[18] *S.Z.*, p. 324.
[19] *S.Z.*, p. 324.

In this light, therefore, the question about the meaning of care is a question about the dimension of the project which makes care as care possible. To bring to light the dimension of a project is precisely to disclose what makes this project as such possible.

As we have seen in the foregoing, the meaning of care can become clear only in the perspective of death. At the moment when *Dasein* understands death as its ultimate possibility, i.e., as a possibility which makes its being impossible, and at the moment when it accepts and recognizes this final possibility as its very own, *Dasein* becomes transparent to itself as a personal be-ing, i.e., in its self. For death does not just appear to *Dasein* in an undifferentiated way, but lays claim to it as an individual *Dasein*.[20] By really understanding death and by accepting it as its own death, *Dasein* breaks away from inauthentic being and throws itself into its authentic being.

The Future

This anticipating of death by including death in advance in every project also has the character of receiving because precisely in this way *Dasein* receives its foundation, i.e., it returns to its own foundation. By anticipating death, *Dasein* receives its being precisely as its own, as its ownmost personal existence, so that it really comes to be itself. This is what Heidegger calls "future" (*Zu-kunft*) in the most primordial sense of the term: "This letting itself come toward itself in that distinctive possibility which [*Dasein*] puts up with, is the primordial phenomenon of the future" (*Zu-kunft*="coming toward").[21] In this sense, *Dasein* is the bearer of the future.

Obviously, Heidegger's view of the future differs fundamentally from the usual conception of the future and of time in general. Here on this point, as everywhere else in *Being and Time,* Heidegger attempts to show how the

---

[20]*S.Z.,* p. 263.
[21]*S.Z.,* p. 325.

future, past, present and time are primordially meaningful for man and how, from this primordial meaning, the current conception could develop. According to Heidegger, the general conception of time is the vision of "fallen" man, which has later been idealized by science. "Fallen" man does not wonder about the conditions that make time possible. For the man in the street, time is an obscure power which continuously makes short moments of "now" reach the present from the future, thereby making them real, and then driving them at once into the past by constantly bringing forward new moments of "now."

Primordially, however, the future (*Zu-kunft*) does not mean a "now" which has not yet become "real" but which will be real at some time, but "the coming (*Kunft*) in which *Dasein*, in its ownmost power to be, comes toward (*zu*) itself."[22] Anticipating death makes *Dasein* authentically futural ("coming toward"), insofar as *Dasein* as being-in-the-world is always coming toward itself already, i.e., coming toward its own being.

One who habitually makes a sharp distinction between the different phases of temporal succession will inevitably get lost here, since Heidegger makes the ecstases of time encompass each other primordially in a reciprocal implication. Let us develop this point a little more in detail.

The Future and "Having Been"

Dasein's temporality extends not only to the future but also to the "having been." *Dasein* can project itself toward its own death only insofar as it already is. In order to realize my own being, I have to accept, together with my death, also my "being thrown," i.e., what I already am. Death cannot be my death if it has no relation to what *Dasein* already is: "Authentically futural, *Dasein is* authentically 'having been.' To anticipate one's ultimate and ownmost possibility is to come back understandingly to one's ownmost 'having been.' "[23]

---

[22]*S.Z.*, p. 325.
[23]*S.Z.*, p. 326.

The future, then, is in a certain sense the genuine completion of the "having been"; it supposes the past but, again, this past cannot manifest itself unless there is a future. Hence there exists a relationship of reciprocal implication between past and future. Thus, in Heidegger's view all phases of time exist together in the present. We can separate them from one another only by applying the external framework of worldly time to them, but this application is only a projection of *Dasein's* real time upon the objects of the world. On the other hand, past, present and future do not constitute a homogenous and undifferentiated mass; but the phases of time must be distinguished without annihilating time's unity. The phases of time imply one another and nonetheless are mutually exclusive. For this reason Heidegger calls them "ec-static," but it is precisely this mutual exclusion that constitutes the typical bond of time. "Temporality is the primordial 'outside of itself' in and for itself."[24]

"Having Been" and the Past

In the preceding paragraphs we spoke occasionally of "having been" instead of "past." Heidegger expressly distinguishes between "having-beenhood" (*Gewesenheit*) and "past" (*Vergangenheit*). The last term indicates the past in the usual sense of the word, in which time is considered to be a pure sequence of moments, and the past is the sum total of the "nows" that are no more. If, however, time is nothing "outside" *Dasein,* in other words, if *Dasein* itself temporalizes, itself is time, then there must also be a past that is distinct from the past in the accepted sense of the word. This past of which *Dasein* can claim that it is its own is the "having been." This "having been" is not something distinct from me; it is what I have been and what I still am in some way; it is that which, having been, is still present, that which is present *as* having been.

---

[24]*S.Z.*, p. 329.

In the accepted view, the past is a "now that is gone," but for Heidegger it is a "gone that is still here." The "having been" is the past as characteristic of *Dasein*. *Dasein,* however, begins by understanding itself in terms of intraworldly be-ings, non-human be-ings. Thus it understands its own "having been" as a series of "nows" that are past. In other words, it understands its own temporality by way of analogy with the temporality of things.

Heidegger adds[25] and explains in detail that *Dasein's* "having been" far exceeds a person's own life. *Dasein's* essential historicity manifests itself here. If we want to understand our world, we must take into account also other periods of history in which ours was molded. Through history, which hitherto has been able to throw only a very defective light on everything that has preceded our existence, *Dasein* comes in contact with the "having been" in the most general sense of the word.

"Making Present"

So far we have spoken almost exclusively about the future and the "having been," without paying much attention to temporal nearness, to the present. According to Heidegger, the meaning of the present lies in "making present" (*Gegenwärtigen*). *Dasein,* as temporalizing, makes be-ings present; this is the essential feature of the present as it primordially appears to *Dasein*. "Anticipating resoluteness discloses the current situation of the *Da* in such a way that existence, in its action, is circumspectively concerned with what is factually 'ready to hand' in the surroundings. Resolute being 'at' what is 'ready to hand' in the situation, that is, actively letting that which has environmental presence be encountered, is possible only by *making* such a be-ing present."[26]

---

[25]*S.Z.,* II, 5, pp. 372-404.
[26]*S.Z.,* p. 326.

The "making present" of what has presence presupposes, on the one hand, the future as anticipation of *Dasein's* possibilities and, on the other, the return to what "has been." By virtue of *Dasein's* understanding of its own being, therefore, *Dasein* can understand the human situation as a whole, and intraworldly be-ings can manifest themselves to it in their belonging to the world. This is what Heidegger calls "making present," which presupposes therefore the "having been" and the future. The present is as a resultant of the two other ecstases of time. "Having been" arises from the future, and in such a way that the future which "has already been" releases the present from itself. What is meant by temporality is precisely the unity of this structured whole: the future which "makes present" in the process of "having been." Only insofar as *Dasein* is characterized by temporality can it realize its authentic being. Temporality here reveals itself as the meaning of authentic care.[27]

Dasein's Temporality and Care

We can now answer our original question of how *Dasein* as care can realize the total unity of its own being and how care can be this unifying basis: *Dasein* can realize its total unity only by temporalizing itself. This "becoming temporal" includes at the same time future, "having been" and present. We must now investigate what the relations are which connect these ecstases of time with the structural elements of care. As was said previously, the primordial structure of care can be expressed as "having to be 'ahead of itself,'" while being-in-a-world and being absorbed in intraworldly be-ings." Thus the relation should be immediately clear. "The 'ahead of itself' [existentiality] is grounded in the future. The 'being already in . . .'" [facticity] makes known the 'having been.' 'Being at' ["fallenness"] becomes possible in 'making present.'"[28]

---

[27]*S.Z.*, p. 326.
[28]*S.Z.*, p. 327.

In this passage Heidegger appears to proceed as follows. He begins with the analysis of the fundamental elements of *Dasein* as being-in-the-world; these existentialia are primordial understanding, fundamental mood and logos. Each existentiale reveals in its own way *Dasein's* own being. Primordial understanding discloses *Dasein's* being as existence, the fundamental mood discloses *Dasein* as "being thrown" and facticity, and logos brings "fallen" being to light. The unity of these three fundamental elements is constituted by care. Thus we see that existence is founded in the future, facticity in "having been," and discursive "falling" in the present. Heidegger himself formulates their connection explicitly in this way.[29]

Accordingly, there are relations of reciprocal implication between the three ecstases of time. They do not lie alongside one another but are together. One of these ecstases can play a dominant role in this totality of mutually inclusive elements. In that case the dominant ecstasis determines the authenticity or inauthenticity of *Dasein's* temporalization. The reason is that the three ecstases of time are connected with the three fundamental existentialia, which can be realized either authentically or inauthentically.

Authentic and Inauthentic Future

How are the authentic forms of time's ecstases contrasted with the inauthentic forms? The authentic future is the anticipation of *Dasein's* ultimate potentiality, viz., death. In this anticipation of death, *Dasein* reaches authentic being; it lets itself come toward itself as its ultimate power to be. In the inauthentic future, *Dasein* understands its own being in terms of the objects of its concernful dealing with intraworldly be-ings. *Dasein* is then directed to everyday things and events, to the objects of its everyday concern. Heidegger calls this being directed to the objects of concern, "awaiting (*Gewärtigen*). This "tending" to intraworldly be-ings opens to *Dasein* a cer-

[29]*S.Z.*, pp. 327-328.

tain perspective upon what it can expect. This "tending" makes the expecting possible, and the expecting in its turn is connected with the future. For expecting presupposes that one can transcend the present and "tending" provides leeway for expecting. Accordingly, *Dasein* transcends the present even in the inauthentic future.[30]

Authentic and Inauthentic Present

Because the future can exist in neither one nor the other of these two modes without the two other ecstases of time, we must see how the authentic and the inauthentic forms of time are contrasted in the present and the past.

Regarding the present, Heidegger describes its authentic form as follows. To being "ahead of itself" there corresponds a certain form of being present, in which there is no longer question of being absorbed in the immediate object of our concernful dealing with things, but which is connected with the authentic future and the authentic "having been." "The present which is held in authentic temporality and which therefore is itself authentic we call the 'glance of the eyes'" (*Augenblick*).[31] The "glance of the eyes" as ecstasis of time is not a moment of time, not a "present now" before which things pass, but it is precisely that which "makes present" and therefore makes it possible to encounter things. In contrast with the "glance of the eyes" as the authentic present, stands the inauthentic "presentation." Both "make present," but not in the same way. The "glance of the eyes" opens what is being made present and thus makes it possible for *Dasein* to be simultaneously in the future and in the "having been" and to understand what is being made present. "Presentation," on the other hand, is insatiable curiosity, which constantly feeds on what is present without really understanding it. Curiosity therefore characterizes the inauthentic present.

---

[30]*S.Z.*, p. 337.
[31]*S.Z.*, p. 338. *Augenblick* is usually translated as "moment," but its literal sense is "glance of the eyes." (Tr.)

Authentic "Having Been" and Inauthentic Past

In relation to what is gone, Heidegger opposes "having been" to the past (*Vergangenheit*) in the ordinary sense of the word. Re-trieving (*Wieder-holung*) former possibilities is essential to "having been." "Having been" does not even mean "gone forever," for we do not definitely leave it behind but always have to return to it and thus keep it present. If we want to realize our own being, we have to come back to what is gone because it already contains our own being in a certain sense. In the inauthentic past one lets what is gone slip away and forgets about it. Thus one also forgets oneself, for one's "having been" cannot be distinguished from one's *Dasein*. *Dasein* is its "having been," even if it has forgotten the meaning of it. When *Dasein* forgets its "having been," it concentrates on its concern with intrawordly be-ings that are present now by re-taining them. Thus, the inauthentic past is pre-eminently re-tention; holding on to what is "merely there" is the consequence of forgetting oneself. All other forms of forgetting, such as forgetting a name, an order, or a date, are only secondary forms of this primordial self-for-getting. In inauthentic being *Dasein* is not conscious of its self-forgetfulness.[32]

These few remarks are far from exhausting the wealth of thought which Heidegger offers in a rather compli-cated form. We only mentioned what seemed necessary to understand the broad lines of his thinking. It has been shown, at least, that time is not a be-ing. Time is not something which belongs externally to all events and thus provides a general frame in which all events can take place. *Dasein* itself is primordially temporalizing. Then, if *Dasein's* being realizes itself in temporality, and if the different ways of being are only different modes of tem-poralizing, and if, on the other hand, there exists an essen-tial relation between *Dasein* and being as such, one sus-pects that there must be an essential connection between

[32]*S.Z.*, p. 339.

time and being. In the title of Heidegger's book *Being and Time,* the particle "and" does not indicate an arbitrary connection as if these two are merely juxtaposed. On the contrary, the "and" is intended to indicate the very fundamental connection between time and being, which the Greeks had already suspected, but which was first expressly thematized in Heidegger's work.

4. A FEW COMPLEMENTARY REMARKS

What Heidegger writes about temporality, ecstases of time and time itself seems very strange to those who are unfamiliar with contemporary philosophy. First of all, one is surprised to see that time has become a central theme of ontology since for many centuries the philosophical study of time was a part of the philosophy of nature. Secondly, one cannot fail to notice that what Heidegger writes about temporality and time differs greatly from what is usually called time.

Time in Metaphysics

As far as the first difficulty is concerned, many philosophers since Hegel have transferred time from philosophy of nature to metaphysics or ontology. Together with Hegel, they attribute to time a function that corresponds closely to the function of being in traditional metaphysics. One can name here Marx, Bergson, Lavelle, Husserl, Merleau-Ponty and others. Heidegger, therefore, is not alone in viewing time as he does. Undoubtedly his ideas about time are connected with those of Hegel and certainly those of Husserl.

Also, caution must be taken to remember that time as considered by Heidegger is totally different from the time defined by Aristotle as "the number of motion according to before and after." The amazement which arises when one becomes acquainted for the first time with Heidegger's ideas about time will probably disappear as soon as one begins to understand what exactly he means by temporality and time.

The Old Concept of Time

Concerning the second difficulty, one should keep in mind that temporality is usually understood as the transitoriness of finite be-ings, while time is generally spoken of as that by which the changes of things can be measured and dated. This pre-philosophical conception of temporality and time can be found in a more developed form throughout the history of philosophy. Aristotle's definition tries to give a precise description of time as the measurement of motion and change. The concept of time, which since Newton has often been proposed, is derived from that of Aristotle by idealizing and hypostatising. It makes time a one-dimensional continuum which exists independently of and outside things and man, and in which all phenomena and events have to take a fixed and *a priori* predictable place by virtue of a universal causal determinism.

In addition to this conception of time, there are others which in one way or another are deduced from our experience of temporal things. For instance, following Locke and Hume, empiricism speaks of the stream of consciousness. Here time is the essence itself of man's inner conscious life, which is nothing but a merging succession of moments of consciousness or contents of consciousness that are separate but connected through association.

Contemporary philosophers do not simply reject these concepts of time, but they do maintain that none of them can be regarded as the primary idea of time, i.e., as a direct expression of our first, primordial experience of time, and therefore as a first expression of what time essentially is. All of them are derivative conceptions which presuppose more or less complex interference of man with the primordial datum. If one wants to discover what time essentially is, one will have to return to the most primordial experience of time that man knows, or better yet, to the pre-ontological knowledge which is contained in the existential experience of our being-man itself.

Time as Presence

According to Heidegger and many other contemporary thinkers, our primordial experience of time contains not only a certain experience of transitoriness, of succession and of continuous flux, but also and even primarily an experience of presence. What we call the "past" is something which was once present to us and which is regarded as past from the standpoint of our "now" but is still retained as such by retention. What we call the "future" is something which we anticipate from our present, something which we expect as a possibility that can or will ever become a present reality.

Accordingly, at the root of the ideas "past" and "future" there is the experience of presence to us. Time is always and essentially presence to us; it is even the only mode of presence which man knows, viz., the finite presence, which is a dialectics of absence and presence in which the negativity of absence is part of the basis of the positivity of presence. The experience of existence which is what makes us men and which permits us to experience ourselves, to maintain and to realize ourselves together with others in the world, is an experience of time. That is, it is an experience of presence which essentially shows an ecstatic temporal structure, and which needs the negativity of the past and the future in order to be able to encounter and to recognize reality as such.

For what do we call real? In contradistinction to the unreal images of dreams we call real what appears to us as a junction of facticity and meaning, i.e., as something which we encounter in an experience of presence as "already there" but at the same time as the object of possible projects for me and for others, and finally as a meeting place for a possible encounter with others in a common task. Reality therefore is for man the noematic correlate of our encounter, of an experience of presence, whose essence contains a reference to both the past and the future.

What applies to real things, applies *a fortiori* to the world as the horizon of all be-ings. The world, as the cradle of all concrete be-ings, is a structured totality of situations and tasks, and as such is the noematic correlate of our temporalizing and historizing existence. Hence the world is not an orderless or orderly sum total of things, but the place where man lives, where he has a task to fulfill, and where he has to make an issue of his being as a "having to be" and as "being with."

Being and Time

Our experience of existence makes us present in being and constitutes us as man. This experience gives us the possibility to live and to act as genuinely human be-ings, to encounter reality together with others and to deal with this reality in an intelligent and meaningful way, to bring our own manhood and that of others to a higher level through this meaningful association and to liberate it. From the preceding pages it follows that this experience of existence is essentially an experience of time which not only has time as its object but which even constitutes temporality and is constituted by temporality. For man to be means to exist, to be-in-the-world. This experience of presence which finds itself in the world and is attuned to the world is an experience of time. Temporality is for man the typical way in which he is present in being, in which he "stands" in being and in which he vouches for and even is responsible for the disclosure of being. Temporality is for man the source of all understanding of being, the "place" from where all human understanding originates.

These remarks, which closely follow Dondeyne's reflections,[33] do not solve all problems. The last word about

---

[33]"Philosophie van de tijd en metaphysica," *Tijdschrift* v. *Philosophie,* vol. XXI (1959), pp. 491-517.

the essence of time has not been spoken. According to Heidegger, a definitive answer is not even possible as long as the question about Being itself is not brought closer to a solution, because it is exactly from time that being can be unconcealed.[34] Time is connected with being because it is connected with being's unconcealment and therefore also with the truth of being. Not without reason does the Preface of *Being and Time* end with this remarkable sentence: "In the following treatise we intend to work out the question of the meaning of being in a concrete fashion. Our provisional aim is to interpret time as the possible horizon for any understanding whatsoever of being."[35]

---

[34]*Was ist Metaphysik?*, p. 17.
[35]*S.Z.*, p. 1.

CHAPTER EIGHT

REALITY AND TRUTH

1. REALITY

Heidegger concludes his introductory analysis of human existence with a study of reality and truth. Because his analytics of *Dasein* is intended to prepare the ontological question regarding the meaning of being, it is important to draw attention to this ontological perspective, which was not sufficiently emphasized in the preceding chapters. Heidegger's reflections on reality and truth seem very well suited for this purpose.[1]

The Priority of the Thing

In traditional metaphysics, the understanding of being was, according to Heidegger, oriented one-sidedly to the being of intraworldly be-ings. Moreover, too much attention was paid to "what is present at hand" (*Vorhandenes*) —to such an extent that be-ing was readily identified with "thing" (*res*). Thus being acquired the sense of "reality" (a term derived from *res*). Since *Dasein* was considered in the same perspective, it was conceived like all other be-ings, as "real" and "merely present at hand."[2] In this way the concept "reality" received a peculiar priority over all other concepts in ontological problematics.

This priority, in its turn, had several other important consequences for traditional metaphysics. They are: 1) *Dasein's* own being could no longer be correctly understood; 2) the problematics of being was forced into an entirely wrong direction because traditional metaphysics did not start from a primordial datum.

---

[1] *S.Z.*, pp. 182-183.
[2] *S.Z.*, p. 201.

Consciousness and Being "in Itself"

Moreover, in the problem of reality several questions were mixed and thereby confused: 1) Those be-ings which supposedly transcend consciousness, *are* they at all? 2) Can the reality of the "outside world" be sufficiently proved? 3) To what extent can man know such be-ings, as real be-ings, in their being in themselves? 4) What is the most profound meaning of this be-ing called "reality"?

The last of these questions is ontologically the most important. However, in the absence of a pure ontological problematics and method, it was in fact always confounded with the first and second questions. For the analysis of reality can be made only when a suitable approach to reality is found. For a long time this approach was sought by contemplative theoretical knowledge. Insofar as the characteristics of being "in itself" and independence are essential for all reality, the question of the meaning of reality became linked with that of whether reality can be independent of consciousness, in other words, whether consciousness can transcend itself and reach reality.

It stands to reason, however, that the possibility of adequately analyzing the meaning of reality depends upon the question to what extent consciousness itself, of which reality is to be independent and which therefore has to be transcended, has been clarified in its own being. Strictly speaking, there are two problems that must be answered before one can ask the question regarding the ultimate meaning of reality: 1) What is knowing? 2) Is knowing an approach and *a fortiori the* privileged approach to being?[3]

The "Outside World"

Traditional philosophy divorces the knower from the known in the problem of knowledge. It is not difficult to understand that anyone who takes this position sooner or later has to face the critical problem, as it was for the first time sharply formulated by Descartes. For, one who

---

[3] *S.Z.,* pp. 200-202.

makes the world independent from the knower necessarily isolates man completely. If one then speaks of our knowledge of the world, one has to consider this knowledge as a certain process which occurs "inside" man. Thus one is immediately confronted with the question of how one can show that this process "inside" man can give reliable knowledge about the "outside world." The existence of this world, moreover, is simply postulated without any justification whatsoever.

On the other hand, if knowing is viewed as a way of being-in-the-world, it does not have to be interpreted as a process in which the subject makes "representations" that are kept "inside" himself. And the question of how these "representations" can agree with reality then becomes a meaningless question.[4] Moreover, the question of whether there really is a world and whether its reality can be proved becomes, likewise, meaningless as a question asked by *Dasein* as being-in-the-world. And who else but *Dasein* could possibly ask this question or try to answer it?

The confusion of what one wants to prove with what one does prove, and with the means to carry out the proof, manifests itself very clearly in Kant's *Refutation of Idealism*. According to Kant, it is a scandal of philosophy that the cogent proof for the existence of things outside us has not yet been delivered. But for Heidegger, the basic error of all attempts to find such a proof lies in the fact that they start from the supposition that man is originally "worldless" and that he therefore has to assure himself somehow of the world's existence in and through philosophy. Being-in-the-world then becomes something that is based on opinion, reasoning, belief or some kind of "already knowing," whereas all knowledge is precisely a mode of *Dasein,* based on being-in-the-world.

Accordingly, the problem of reality as the question of whether there is an "outside world" reveals itself as an

---

[4] *S.Z.,* p. 62.

impossible question—not because its consequences lead to insurmountable difficulties, but because the be-ings themselves considered in that question exclude such a problematics. One does not have to prove that and how there is an "outside world," but one has to explain why *Dasein* as being-in-the-world tends first to "bury" the "outside world" epistemologically and then to prove its existence. Heidegger thinks that the explanation is to be found in *Dasein's* "fallenness," for in this "fallenness" *Dasein's* primary understanding of being is diverted to be-ings as "already there."[5]

Realism and Idealism

Heidegger's standpoint agrees with that of realism insofar as it does not deny in any way that intraworldly be-ings are there, but it disagrees insofar as realism thinks that the reality of the world can and must be proved. In principle, Heidegger even has a measure of preference for the standpoint of idealism because idealism clearly realizes that being cannot be explained in terms of be-ings. However, even though being cannot be explained in terms of be-ings, we still have the obligation to investigate the being of consciousness, the question of the being of the *res cogitans*. Only because being is "in consciousness," i.e., is understandable in *Dasein,* can *Dasein* understand and conceptualize such characteristics as the independence of being, its "in itself," and reality in general.

If, then, idealism amounts to realizing that being cannot be explained in terms of be-ings, but is "transcendental" for every be-ing, then idealism offers the only possibility to posit the problem in a genuinely philosophical way. In that case Aristotle was just as much an idealist as Kant. If, on the other hand, idealism amounts to reducing all being to a subject or a consciousness, then idealism is just as naive as the most superficial brand of realism.[6]

5*S.Z.*, pp. 203-206.
6*S.Z.*, pp. 206-208.

Reality and Care

Accordingly, we must conclude that the problem of reality, no matter how it is approached, is to be included in *Dasein's* existential analysis as an ontological problem and not merely as an epistemological issue. If the term "reality" indicates the being of the intraworldly be-ing, the *res* that is "there,"—and it would be difficult to assign any other sense to it—then, as far as the analysis of *Dasein's* mode of being which is called "knowing" is concerned, this means that the intraworldly be-ing can be ontologically understood only when the phenomenon of the world's worldhood is explained. But this worldhood is based on the phenomenon of the world which, itself, as an essential aspect of the structure of being-in-the-world, belongs to *Dasein's* fundamental constitution. Being-in-the-world, in turn, is ontologically tied up with the structural totality of *Dasein's* being, which we have characterized as care.

These thoughts outline the foundations and horizons which must be clarified if an analysis of "reality" is to be possible.[7] As an ontological term, "reality" refers to worldly being. If it is used only to signify this way of being, then "merely being present at hand" and being "ready to hand" function as the modes of reality. No matter how one conceives the being of "nature," all modes of being of worldly be-ings are ontologically founded in the worldhood of the world and consequently in the phenomenon of being-in-the-world itself.

Thus it follows that reality has no priority among the modes of being of worldly be-ings and that reality is a mode of being which is not even suited to characterize the world and *Dasein*. On the level of the interconnection of things in their ontological foundation and on the level of any possible categorical and existential explicitation, reality refers back to the phenomenon of "care."

---

[7] *S.Z.*, pp. 208-209.

The statement that reality is ontologically rooted in *Dasein's* being does not mean that a worldly be-ing can be what it is in itself only when, and only as long as, a *Dasein* exists. Of course, it is true that only as long as *Dasein is,* i.e., as long as the understanding of being is ontically possible, "is there" (*es gibt*) being. If no *Dasein* exists, "independence" "is" not either, nor "is" there an "in itself." In such a case, this kind of expressions are neither understandable nor not understandable since intraworldly be-ings can then neither be discovered nor lie hidden. In other words, one can say neither that they are nor that they are not.

Accordingly, the dependence of being (*not* of intraworldly be-ings) on the understanding of being, i.e., the dependence of reality (*not* of the real) on care, intends only to express that be-ing as be-ing becomes accessible only when there is understanding of being. But now, since there are in fact be-ings that have *Dasein's* mode of being, the understanding of being is possible as a be-ing.

2. TRUTH

Various Approaches

According to Heidegger, the fundamental question of what truth is can be approached in different ways, depending on one's starting point. Because of the important discoveries that can be made by it, Heidegger has incorporated the most important of these approaches in *Being and Time*. He starts there from what the analytics of man's being had already disclosed and concludes that precisely the phenomenon of truth is that which constitutes man as man. The phenomenological analysis of *Dasein* as being-in-the-world and existence appears to lead of necessity to the essence of truth, and in this essence man's own being finds its radical explanation.

Heidegger comes to the same conclusion in *On the Essence of Truth* by a different and shorter way. Here he starts from the traditional definition of truth as the "conformity of intellect and thing" (*adaequatio intellectus et rei*). After asking what precisely is to be understood by conformity, he tries to determine how, ultimately, this conformity is intrinsically possible. Finally, he attempts to assign a definitive foundation to this possibility.

In his latest works he endeavors to clarify the essence of truth from the history of the "clearing" of "Being" (*Lichtungsgeschichte von "Sein"*),[8] i.e. from the essence of that to which, in the course of history, truth has led in the fields of science, arts, technique, and philosophy.

The reflections on truth contained in *Being and Time* can be interpreted in two entirely different ways. One can conclude that, according to Heidegger, the ultimate foundation of truth lies in *Dasein's* existence. However, reading his text in the perspective which is stongly emphasized in his *Letter on Humanism,* it appears that Being itself is the ultimate foundation of truth, although this point is not yet expressly made in *Being and Time.* Since we will consider this problem later, we will limit ourselves here to Heidegger's position with respect to the traditional concept of truth. The best approach probably is to start with his work *On the Essence of Truth.*

The Classical Definition of Truth

Heidegger argues that since Parmenides philosophy has tried to connect truth closely with being. Aristotle too did not distinguish between searching for truth and investigating being. The famous conception of truth, which is traditionally attributed to Aristotle but seems to have been formulated by Isaac Israeli, can be summarized in the following two theses: 1) the place of truth is judgment; 2) the essence of truth lies in the conformity of judgment and object. According to Heidegger, this conception has been maintained until the present without any serious opposition. Not only did medieval scho-

---

[8]*Identität und Differenz,* p. 47.

lasticism take over this view, but Descartes and Kant also adhered to it, though with some reservations.[9]

Husserl too never doubted the classical definition of truth; he accepted it as correct, although he gave it a completely different interpretation, probably without even being explicitly aware of it. The meaning and function of the classical definition of truth in Husserl's works were entirely different from those it had in classical philosophy, as is evident from the fact that in this matter Husserl did not distinguish between intellectual knowledge and sense knowledge and did not hold that the judgment alone is the "locus" of truth. Of course, Husserl accepted that truth is encountered in the judgment also; but according to him, this judgment is rooted in a prepredicative experience in which the contrast between sense knowledge and intellectual knowledge is transcended and in which the problem of truth announces itself already in a primordial way. According to Husserl, the problem of truth on the level of pre-predicative experience is more complicated because the notions of "presence" and "evidence," which are essentially allied to the notion of truth, are not univocal notions. Nevertheless, he maintained the classical definition of truth on this level also, although, because of the above-mentioned analogy, its sense differs from the one Aristotle gave to it.

Heidegger agrees with the main lines of Husserl's ideas in this matter, but adds that Husserl limited himself to a theory about truth, although an ontology should have been provided as the foundation for this theory. In *On the Essence of Truth* Heidegger says that the crucial problem about truth does not lie in the questions which things, which judgments or which acts are true or in precisely what kinds of truth one has to distinguish from one another. The primary task, he says, is to define truth *as* truth.[10] Undoubtedly, the questions of the different

---

[9] *S.Z.*, pp. 212-215.
[10] *Vom Wesen der Wahrheit*, p. 5.

levels of truth, its eternity, its necessity, its absoluteness or its contingent character are of great importance and have to be discussed in a coherent theory on truth; but all this is not possible until a foundation has been provided by a doctrine of truth as truth.

Starting from the different ways in which man gives expression to the idea of truth, Heidegger concludes that the classical definition of truth is undoubtedly meaningful. Truth is the "conformity between thing and intellect." If one speaks of true gold, one intends to say that a certain piece of metal is really gold, i.e., it corresponds to the notion which we have formed about genuine gold (conformity of thing with intellect). We call a judgment true when it corresponds to the thing which is judged (conformity of the intellect with the thing). In this way Heidegger accepts the scholastic view of ontological truth and logical or epistemological truth. According to scholasticism, all knowledge has to be in harmony with the things, and these, in the last analysis, have to be in harmony with the ideas God had about them when He created them. Hence ontological truth has to be connected with logical truth. However, one should keep in mind that in these two cases there is question of different intellects and, strictly speaking, also of different things.

Later the reference to the divine intellect was omitted, but otherwise the scholastic opinion was maintained in its original form. Kant and Hegel also spoke about logical truth as conformity of the intellect with the thing, and about ontological truth as conformity of the thing with the intellect. According to Kant, the truth of the object is constituted by transcendental subjectivity, while our empirical knowledge is governed by the objects. In Hegel these two aspects of truth became inseparable and one is only an abstract phase of the other. Yet the idea of conformity continued to define the essence of truth.[11]

---

[11]*Ibid.*, pp. 5-9.

Ontological Foundation of Truth

If, as is generally done, one conceives consciousness here as identical with presentation, the problems become insoluble, as is clear from the history of epistemology. Husserl was right when he argued that the classical definition of truth is meaningful only when one regards consciousness as intentionality. Yet Husserl did not go far enough because in the last analysis it is impossible to define truth in any way whatsoever without implying an interpretation of the being of be-ings. If one does not accurately indicate what intellect (=*Dasein*) and thing (*res*) are in themselves, any theory of truth remains empty and certainly without a radical foundation.[12] Moreover, the classical conception of truth contains a series of implicit positions regarding untruth and error, which should be made explicit and justified. In this sense the classical theory of truth, even as corrected by Husserl, requires an ontology of truth.[13] This ontology can best be presented by starting from the classical conception of truth.

What exactly is meant by the conformity upon which the classical view rests? Its explanation will immediately lead us to the ontological presuppositions upon which this view is based.

The conformity in question is obviously an analogous notion. We say, for example, that two silver dollars are equal or in conformity with each other; in my true judgment I am in conformity with the object of my judgment. In the first case there is a conformity between two objects based upon their participation in one and the same form. In the second case there is no question of two material objects, but of one material object and a statement about it. How then can we speak here of conformity? One can say that the judgment refers "itself" to the piece

---

[12]*Ibid.*, p. 9.
[13]*Ibid.*

of money insofar as the judgment re-presents the object, under a certain aspect, as it is.[14]

Closer investigation, however, shows that this re-presenting has nothing to do with a representation by means of signs or image (*repraesentatio*), but means that one places a thing as it is before oneself (*appraesentatio*). In the judgment I "intend" and aim at something other than the I. In this "intending," this other, to the extent that it is "tended to," and under the formal aspect in which it is "tended to," is presented by me to myself and finds itself before me, that is, it is constituted an object. This objectivation is not the same in all cases; but it varies according to the different kinds of judgments. This point, however, need not concern us at present.

Every judgment and every statement related to a reality which they re-present as it is call forth a special form of human behavior which characterizes man's way of being and distinguishes man's being from that of all other be-ings. This behavior is essentially tied up with reality in an intentional and transcendental way. But one cannot give a meaning to the real if it is not first made present to man and if man has not placed it before himself and if he does not let it rise before him. This, however, presupposes that man is openness both to things and to himself, i.e., that man is *Dasein*, being-in-the-world, existence. In this perspective re-presentation, as a supposedly essential element of every form of knowledge, makes no sense at all. Thus we see that Heidegger expressly returns here to Husserl's idea of intentionality, but interprets it in an entirely different way.[15]

Truth and Freedom

Accordingly, Heidegger accepts the correctness of the classical definition of truth as Husserl tried to interpret it,

---

[14]*Ibid.*, pp. 10-11.
[15]*Ibid.*, pp. 10-12.

but he claims that this view of truth necessarily implies a certain vision of the being of man. He attempts to clarify this vision first,[16] and goes on to draw attention to other aspects of the question.

If it is true that our judgments are directed to the things about which they want to say something, then one has to ask why our judgments, as well as our entire knowledge, can and must accept the real as their norm. Why does man "consent" to adjust himself radically to things in his knowledge, his action and his whole behavior? Why does he subject himself to the things in order to derive from them the substance and value of what he knows and does?

Strictly speaking, one should not pose the problem this way, for we face the *fact* that man does obey the real and that things do constitute the norm governing his knowledge and his behavior. It is better therefore to ask under what conditions such an attitude is possible. The answer is that it is possible because man is free. For, if our behavior adjusts itself to things, if it meets them as they are, then "things as they are" have to be the norm governing the "open" be-ing which faces them. Remaining what they are, things present themselves as they are, and this within the domain of that "open" whose openness is not created by *Dasein's* re-presentation, but merely is taken over by it as a possible referential system. This "open" is for Heidegger the world as the necessary horizon within whose limits every concrete be-ing can be truly brought to light by man. Man is essentially and primordially related to this always already given "open," the world, and in each concrete form of behavior this fundamental relation is, as it were, actualized.[17] In this actualization man relates himself to be-ings which as being-present, as manifest, are experienced as such. "What is thus, and solely in the strict sense, made manifest was experienced early in

[16]*S.Z.*, pp. 212-220.
[17]*Vom Wesen der Wahrheit*, p. 11.

Western thought as 'that which is present' (*ousia*) and has long been called 'be-ing.' "[18]

Because man is openness to himself and to the world as the "open," and ultimately because man is primordially openness to Being as the unconcealed, man is able to make particular things manifest as these particular things, that is, as they are. His judgments and the statements following these judgments must be governed by the be-ings that have become manifest in this way. It is clear therefore that neither judgment nor statement can be the original "locus" of truth. The essential "locus" of truth lies in the primordial relation in which be-ing becomes disclosed as it is. *Dasein's* openness is a necessary condition for this primordial relation. This openness must be regarded as the proper characteristic of freedom, so that we can conclude that "the essence of truth is freedom."[19]

In spite of the explanation, this assertion may seem strange. One could say, of course, that man must be free in order to be able to perform a certain action and therefore also free to make a re-presentative statement and thus to agree or to disagree with a "truth." But the above-mentioned assertion claims that freedom is the essence of truth. By essence is meant here the basis of the inner possibility of whatever is accepted and generally admitted as known. But in the idea of freedom one does not think of truth and even less of the essence of truth. Moreover, it seems that, by making freedom the essence of truth, truth is left to man's discretion. Such a surrender of truth to man's discretion fundamentally undermines truth by basing it on the subjectivity of the human subject.

These and other similar objections, however, proceed from assumptions that are foreign to what Heidegger really wants to say. The reason for the confusion lies in the fact that the objectors tenaciously cling to certain

---

[18]*Ibid.*
[19]*Ibid.,* p. 12.

prejudices concerning the essence of freedom. They assume that freedom is primordially a characteristic of man, that the essence of freedom is immediately evident, and that everyone knows at once what man is. One of these prejudices needs to be examined more closely here.[20]

The Essence of Freedom

The term "freedom" is generally taken to mean the possibility to choose, "the random ability to go this way or that in our choice."[21] Although it cannot be denied that freedom is to be found also in that choice, the essence of freedom does not lie there. Freedom means essentially the absence of necessity together with a certain autonomy. Freedom means primordially that way of being which enables man to liberate himself from "nature's" grasp. This negative aspect of freedom, however, contains also a positive side. In my power to escape from the grasp of facticity, the positive possibility of my fundamental openness reveals itself equiprimordially and, by virtue of this openness, I can orientate myself to the world and to my own possibilities in regard to intraworldly things. Thus freedom is primordially not a characteristic of human activity, but, as being-in-the-world, man is openness, he transcends being-necessitated and has the positive possibility to transcend and to project. Primordially, therefore, freedom indicates the being of man on the proper level of his manhood.

Dasein and Truth

To explain the bond between truth and freedom, let us now return to what we have already seen. With Heidegger we saw that the classical definition of truth should not be denied, but needs to be given an ontological foundation.

---

[20]*Ibid.*, pp. 12-13.
[21]*Ibid.*, p. 15.

The "locus" of truth is not primordially in the judgment[22] but in man's existence itself. The conformity of judgment with reality presupposes that reality has been drawn from concealment. For this purpose a certain light is needed, the light of human existence which itself is openness. "Insofar as *Dasein is* its disclosedness essentially and, as disclosed, discloses and uncovers it is essentially 'true.' "[23] On the proper level of being-man itself, man is openness and a light to himself; but equiprimordially he is openness and light with respect to other things.[24] As existence, man is a "natural light."[25] Primordially disclosed, man as existence is equiprimordially disclosing and thereby giving rise to meaning.

The truth of the judgment presupposes truth as unconcealedness of be-ings and the truth of human existence as that which dis-covers things; and these two presuppose man's fundamental openness. Hence, the truth of judgment ultimately presupposes that man is "in the truth."[26] "What is primarily 'true'—that is, un-covering—is *Dasein*."[27] The task of *Dasein* lies in "taking be-ings out of their concealedness and letting them be seen in their unconcealedness (their un-coveredness)."[28]

The untruth of judgment can also be considered in the same sense. The being untrue of a judgment presupposes man's being untrue, i.e., the being uprooted of his existence.[29] This "being uprooted" means that man no longer stands in truth as unconcealedness, but stands in "semblance" (*Schein*). Reality does not remain completely concealed here but, although it is to some extent disclosed, it is distorted in one way or another.[30] Thus, the untrue

---

[22]*Ibid.*, pp. 6-9.
[23]*S.Z.*, p. 221
[24]*S.Z.*, pp. 220, 133.
[25]*S.Z.*, p. 133.
[26]*S.Z.*, p. 221.
[27]*S.Z.*, p. 220.
[28]*S.Z.*, p. 219.
[29]*S.Z.*, p. 222.
[30]*S.Z.*, p. 222.

judgment merely explicitates *Dasein's* "standing in semblance."

"Subjectivity" of Truth

Truth in the most primordial sense of the word is therefore an existentiale of *Dasein.* Thus we must conclude: *"Dasein,* as constituted by disclosedness, is essentially in the truth. Disclosedness is a mode of being that is essential to *Dasein.* 'There is' (*es gibt*) truth only insofar as *Dasein is* and so long as *Dasein is.* Be-ings are dis-covered only when *Dasein is;* and are disclosed only as long as it *is."*[31]

Does it follow from this that all truth is merely subjective? If by "subjective" one intends to convey the idea that all truth, by virtue of its own essential way of being, is relative to *Dasein's* being, then this question must undoubtedly be answered in the affirmative. If, however, "subjective" is taken to mean "left to the subject's discretion," then the answer is certainly negative, because "dis-covering . . . places the dis-covering *Dasein* face to face with be-ings themselves."[32] Dis-covery aims precisely at things as they are, and every judgment and statement likewise aims at these things as they are. The "intended" be-ing itself shows itself as it is in itself, i.e., it shows "that it, in its selfsameness, is just as it gets pointed out, dis-covered, in the statement as being.[33] As existence man discloses reality itself, he lets things be for himself as they are.

"Letting Be"

"Letting be" sometimes means that one wants to renounce something, but in the present context it means precisely the opposite. "Letting be" here means to let things be as they are. It implies also that one wishes to have

---

[31]*S.Z.*, p. 226.
[32]*S.Z.*, p. 227.
[33]*S.Z.*, p. 218.

something to do with things, not in order to protect, culti-
vate or conserve them, but only to let them truly be what
they are. This "letting be" takes things from concealedness, it brings them to light and makes them participate in
the truth of being.[34] This "having something to do with
be-ings" in order to bring them to light does not become
absorbed in be-ings. On the contrary, it unfolds itself precisely in making room for be-ings in order that they can
reveal themselves as what they are themselves and precisely as they are, and in order that subsequently our
judgments and statements can find their norm in them.

If both truth and freedom are nothing but expressions
of man's own being on the proper level of his manhood,
then it is evident that the essence of truth can lie precisely in freedom as openness. "The essence of freedom,
seen from the viewpoint of the essence of truth, shows
itself as the 'bringing out' of be-ings into unconcealedness."[35] It also becomes evident then that the "locus"
of truth is not in the judgment, but in that which precisely makes judgments and statements possible, i.e., in
primordial understanding and fundamental "mood."[36]

These few remarks about reality and truth are not ex-
haustive. At this point of our analysis it is not yet possible
to offer definitive solutions of both problems. Such solutions become possible only after the basic problem of
ontology, the question of the meaning of Being itself, has
been solved. We will therefore have to return to them
later.

---

[34]*Vom Wesen der Wahrheit,* pp. 14-15.
[35]*Ibid.,* p. 15.
[36]*Ibid.,* pp. 18-19.

CHAPTER NINE

THE TRANSITION FROM CONCERNFULLY DEALING WITH THINGS TO A SCIENTIFIC APPROACH

The prevalent world view in our contemporary Western civilization is largely controlled by the sciences. A philosophy which wants to make the fundamental philosophical problems its theme in an up-to-date way that appeals to modern man can hardly afford to ignore the phenomenon "science." For this reason Heidegger deals repeatedly and extensively with the fundamental problem that the sciences represent for philosophy.

In these reflections he proves himself a philosopher who is very well informed about several sciences. Before definitely embarking on a philosophical career, Heidegger had spent several years in fruitful studies of mathematics, physics and history.

The main problems which he raises with regard to the sciences are the well-known questions of what science is; how it is constituted; what is to be thought about its truth, certainty and exactness; what relation there exists between science and technique; and especially what should be the relation between philosophy and the non-philosophical sciences.

In *Being and Time* Heidegger deals with the sciences in two different places. In Section Thirteen (pp. 59-62) he writes about our theoretical knowledge and its impact on the positive sciences with the intention of clarifying the "being in" of our being-in-the-world. He tries to throw light on the primordial meaning of "being in" by contrasting our primordial being-in-the-world with our theoretical being-in-the-world and presenting the latter as rooted in and derived from *Dasein's* primordial mode of being-in-the-world. In Section Sixty-Nine (pp. 350-

366) he tries to explain the temporality of being-in-the-world by showing how *Dasein* in its various modes of "being in" is temporal and temporalizing. We will briefly summarize both sections here.

1. THE THEORETICAL MODE OF BEING-IN-THE-WORLD

According to Heidegger, theoretical knowledge, and consequently science also, is a mode of being-in-the-world. A question which imposes itself here immediately is whether this theoretical or scientific mode of being-in-the-world is the primordial mode or merely a derived mode rooted in being-in-the-world. Moreover, we have to search for the existential conditions which make it possible for *Dasein* to exist in the mode of being that characterizes scientific research.[1]

As regards the first question, we have already seen that for Heidegger *Dasein* is essentially being-in-the-world and that this being-in-the-world consists primordially in concernfully dealing with things. Thus the answer to the first question is evident. But we must still show concretely how *Dasein* can proceed from this primordial mode of being-in-the-world to the derived and secondary mode of theoretical being-in-the-world. To clarify this point, Heidegger begins by criticizing the prevalent views concerning theoretical knowledge.

The "Inner" Sphere of the Knower and the "Outer" World

In epistemological treatises it has been common practice to oppose non-knowing nature to knowing man. Knowing as such is not found in nature, and a close observation shows that even in man it is not present in an externally observable way. Consequently, knowing must be found "inside" man. A strong emphasis on this "inside" and a sharp focus on the distinction between knowing, on the one hand, and physical and psychological ways

---

[1] *S.Z.,* p. 357.

of being, on the other, seemed to lead to a certain solution of the question about the nature of knowledge and also of the problem about the relation between "subject" and "object."

However, in this way there arises immediately another question, namely, how the knowing subject can go from its "inner" sphere to the "exterior" sphere in such a way that the subject can know this "exterior" without having to leap into the "other" sphere. The mistake is made of never explicitly asking about the mode of being proper to the knowing subject, although this unstated question is always implied and already implicitly answered somehow. True, we are told sometimes that this "inner" sphere is not a chest for storing the "external world." Nevertheless, no reply is given as to how this sphere has to be understood in a more positive way. Questions are asked about our way of knowing and replies are given, but no attempt is made to reflect radically on what thinking itself is. Yet such a reflection is absolutely necessary.[2]

From "Concernfully Dealing with" to "Merely Whiling"

It is not difficult to show that those problems do not arise at all if the phenomenon of knowing is explicitly taken in the manner in which it primordially presents itself to us, namely, as something that itself is grounded in a "being already in and 'at' the world," which is essentially constitutive of *Dasein's* being. As we have seen, our primordial being-in-the-world can best be characterized as a concernfully dealing with intraworldly be-ings. If, then, knowing is to be possible as a way of determining theoretically what things that are "merely present at hand" are, a "deficiency" must first occur in our concernfully dealing with intrawordly be-ings. By abstaining from any kind of producing, handling and making, primordial concern is reduced to merely "whiling" (*verweilen bei*), which itself also is a mode of being-in-

---

[2]*S.Z.*, pp. 60-61.

the-world. This mode of being with respect to the world lets us encounter the intraworldly be-ing purely in the way it looks (*eidos*). On the basis of this kind of being, and precisely as a mode of it, it is possible to look explicitly at that which is thus encountered.[3]

How exactly does concernfully dealing with things change into looking at in a purely theoretical manner? At first one might be inclined to think that this happens simply because of the fact that one abstains from any kind of concernful dealing with things, from any *praxis*. In that case the origin of the theoretical attitude would consist essentially in the disappearance of *praxis*. For those who consider practical concern the primary and dominating mode of being possessed by concrete man, theory appears to derive its ontological possibility from a *privation;* for when *praxis* disappears, theory remains.

It is hardly necessary to show that this view is wrong. Any *praxis* at times implies such a looking at and, on the other hand, in many instances there can be no theory without *praxis*. It suffices to point to the technical views incorporated in the use of complicated measuring devices in contemporary science. Moreover, the practical handling of intraworldly be-ings requires a certain circumspection, understanding and survey which ultimately become deliberation. It is precisely this "viewing" of things as equipment which must be changed if the theoretical attitude is to arise.

Accordingly, the theoretical attitude does not consist in abandoning *praxis*, but rather in taking a second look at the intraworldly things which our concernful dealing regards as equipment and in conceiving and projecting them as "merely there." The scientific way of looking at the world, then, results from a shift in man's attitude, which fundamentally modifies the primarily given view of the world. The things which initially were handled by man within the framework of his primordial world now

---

[3]*S.Z.,* p. 61.

assume a different character. They lose their location in their original world and henceforth appear only in a place that is unrelated to man and without limitations.[4] "Looking at," which is so characteristic of the theoretical attitude, always implies a certain viewpoint and a new attitude with regard to the things that are present. This attitude in advance makes a certain specific aspect of the thus encountered be-ing the center of our attention.

Dasein as Determiningly Whiling "Outside with"

Knowing is a "dwelling by" which includes a perceiving of, an addressing oneself to, and a discussing of, something as something—briefly, an interpretation in the widest sense. On the basis of this interpretation, perception be-comes making determinate. What is perceived in this way can also be pronounced and preserved in propositions.

This too is a mode of being-in-the-world and need not be interpreted as a "procedure" by which a subject pro-duces "representations" of something which then are stored "inside" and can give rise to the question of how they are in "agreement" with reality. In its turning to something and grasping it, *Dasein* does not first come out of an "inner sphere" as from its shell but, by virtue of its primary mode of being itself, it is always "outside with" an already-encountered be-ing belonging to an already-discovered world. *Dasein* does not leave an "inner sphere" when it "whilingly" is with the be-ings to be known and determines them, but its "being outside with the object" is *Dasein* itself as knowingly being-in-the-world.

Likewise, the perceiving of what is known is not a returning to the "lockers" of consciousness loaded with "booty" after one has gone out to gather knowledge. Even in perceiving, retaining and preserving, the knowing *Dasein* remains "outside" as *Dasein*. Even when I merely know, merely imagine or merely remember some way in which be-ings are interconnected, I am not less with them "out-

---

[4]*S.Z.*, pp. 356-362; 153-160.

side" in the world than I was when I originally perceived them.

By knowing in a theoretical way, *Dasein* achieves a new "state of being" with regard to the world already discovered in *Dasein* itself. This new power to be can develop in an autonomous way, and as science it can even take control over being-in-the-world. The subject's dealing with the world, however, is neither freshly created by theoretical knowledge nor does it originate from an action of the world on the subject. Theoretical knowing is a mode of *Dasein* based upon being-in-the-world itself.[5]

2. THE EXISTENTIAL CONDITIONS OF THE THEORETICAL MODE OF BEING-IN-THE-WORLD

The Temporal Significance of the Transition from Praxis to Theory

The preceding remarks contain also a reply to the question about the existential conditions which make it possible for *Dasein* to exist by way of theoretically knowing. Nevertheless, we have to return to this question to throw light on the temporal significance of the transition from the original *praxis* to theory and science. For this reason we must revert also to what was said about the circumspection which characterizes our everyday dealing with intraworldly be-ings.

As has already been shown, the origin of theory cannot be explained by declaring that theory is what is left when *praxis* is abandoned. One of the reasons why the origin of theory cannot be explained in this way is the fact that *praxis* itself always implies a certain way of viewing intraworldly be-ings, which Heidegger calls "circumspection." According to him, theory arises precisely because this "looking at" intraworldly be-ings itself is changed when there is question of theory.

As has been said repeatedly, circumspection is concerned with the referential relations existing within the equip-

---

[5]*S.Z.*, p. 62.

mental totality. It is guided by a certain "survey" of this totality. The main characteristic of this survey is that it discloses a complex of involvements in which our concernful dealing with things is situated. In other words, this surveying is ultimately a function of the power to be which *Dasein* tries to realize.[6] By interpreting what it has seen through "deliberation," *Dasein's* surveying circumspection brings the intraworldly be-ings within its area of interests.[7]

The scheme according to which this deliberation takes place can be indicated by the conditional relation "if . . . then." For example, *if* this is to happen, *then* that has to be done first; *if* I want to build a house, *then* I must first buy bricks. By such circumspective deliberation *Dasein* becomes clearly aware of its situation in the world. Thus, circumspective deliberation does not intend to establish what the characteristics of things are, but to provide *Dasein* with the possibility of orientating itself within its world. Circumspective deliberation brings things closer to us, it is a way of "making present." This circumspective "making present" has several foundations.

In the first place it presupposes the retention of a certain equipmental context, that is, a temporalization of the past, a bringing back of the past. In its circumspective deliberation *Dasein* is always already with a complex of equipment and materials which it already discovered in its concernful dealing with intraworldly be-ings.

Secondly, *Dasein* looks toward the realization of a certain possibility to which it tends. Thus, whatever *Dasein* does, realizes, or undertakes is conditioned by a "tending to" and is orientated toward an intended possibility. Therefore, the typical "making present" of circumspective deliberation is confined to bringing closer that which is discovered in a retentive "tending to."

Thirdly, the equipment and material needed for doing something must already be known as such. But this know-

[6]*S.Z.*, p. 359.
[7]*S.Z.*, p. 359.

ing likewise implies necessarily a retention and a "tend-ing to": a "tending to" because I can grasp bricks as bricks only in the perspective of the house that will be built of them; a retention because I can link this brick to the house which I intend to build only by returning to past events.

The condition which makes it possible that what has been projected in circumspective understanding can be brought closer in a "making present" lies in the unity of temporalization, i.e., the way the present is rooted in the future and the "having been."[8]

Transition from Praxis to Theory

The importance of all this for the transition from the original *praxis* to theory and science can perhaps best be shown by way of an example. When I say of the hammer which I am using that it is too heavy for me, I want to say that the handling of that hammer requires too much effort. In that case I regard the hammer as a tool which I use within a certain equipmental totality. I can also say, however, that the hammer weighs three pounds. In that case I no longer consider the hammer in function of a definite role within this particular equipmental totality, but as a material thing that is subject to the laws of gravity. Compared to the first sentence, the second sen-tence contains a shift in standpoint: the hammer has been detached from the whole within which it was handled and conceived; it is considered now merely as a material thing which is "simply there."

In this latter perspective it is no longer meaningful to say that the hammer is heavy or light; now the only meaningful statement is the one that expresses precisely how much it weighs. This shift in standpoint is neither the result of the fact that we have actually ceased to wield the hammer nor of the fact that we make abstraction from such possible handling of it. These two aspects are left

---

[8] *S.Z.*, p. 360.

out of consideration in a purely negative way. The only important point is that we have adopted an entirely new attitude with regard to the hammer, in virtue of which we acquire an entirely new view of it. This viewpoint in turn leads to an entirely new type of understanding in which the hammer is regarded solely as a material thing that is "simply there."

Accordingly, there is a change in our understanding of be-ing as be-ing, for the intraworldly be-ing is divorced from its world; it is no longer conceived in its relation to the whole of the surrounding world. When we say that the hammer weighs three pounds, we disregard not only its possible use, but also its location relative to a certain equipmental totality. Its actual and possible location do not matter any more, for the hammer is no longer within the spatial-temporal "world." We can also reverse this and say that its location has become a spatio-temporal moment, a "world point," which is in no way distinguished from any other such point.[9]

In this way the world is being stripped of its spatial determinations. The temporal aspects of the things are also eliminated, since I no longer consider the hammer in the perspective of its use on the basis of an actual situation. The advantage of such procedure is that from now on I am able to describe and determine with precision the structural moments of the "merely there."

3. SCIENTIFIC THINKING AND PHILOSOPHICAL THINKING

Other questions which the philosopher must ask about the sciences can be phrased as follows: What precisely makes a science a science? or How is a science constituted as a science? and What is the relationship between science and philosophy? For practical reasons, let us start with a brief discussion of the last question.

---

[9] *S.Z.*, p. 362.

Martin Heidegger

The Distinction Between Science and Philosophy

According to Heidegger, science and philosophy are essentially different. One of the differences between the two forms of knowing can be found in the fact that sciences do not think radically, while philosophy is characterized precisely by the radicalism of its thinking.

This fundamental difference, which at the same time implies a profound divergence in method, creates an unbridgeable gap between philosophy and science. Any attempt to pass from the one form of knowing to the other runs into insurmountable difficulties because there exists no bridge over this abyss. Switching from philosophy to science or vice versa can be accomplished only by a leap, an abrupt transition by a change in attitude.[10]

Scientists generally interpret this philosophical statement as a disparaging remark which, however, is in no way the intention of the philosophers. Philosophy does not intend to speak against science; on the contrary, it acts in favor of the latter by trying to reach clarity with regard to the true nature of science. Science itself is unable to attain such clarity. For science has another characteristic, which becomes immediately evident when one tries to understand what science is, and which consists in the fact that science cannot turn toward the essence of its own field of study.

For example, the historian who confines himself to purely historical means can never discover what "the historical" in itself is, just as a mathematician is not able to explain the essence of "the mathematical" with purely mathematical means. The essence of its object of study remains hidden from every science. It is the task of philosophy to ask such questions and to seek for their solution. The fact that science itself is unable to deal with the essence of its own objects forces us to say that science cannot think radically.

---

[10]*Was heisst Denken?*, pp. 4-5.

124

Here again philosophy seems to evaluate itself as superior to scientific thinking. We have to take into account, however, that philosophy is well aware of the fact that it has not yet been successful in trying to discover and express the essence of the mathematical, the physical and the historical. Strictly speaking, it knows less in this respect than the sciences, since for centuries the latter have lived up to their name by leading to genuine achievements within the limits imposed upon them.

Nevertheless, it remains true that the sciences are one-sided in the sense that, so long as they remain true to their own character, they are unable to reflect upon the essence of their own objects. The impressive results which the sciences have accomplished within their own domain have often caused scientists to overlook this one-sidedness and thus induced them to usurp the rights of philosophy. Such scientism, however, is entirely unacceptable and untenable because philosophy and science cannot be considered as pursuing the same line.[11]

A third point which strikes our attention in reflecting upon the essence of science is the fact that it always starts from presuppositions which science itself can never justify scientifically. Philosophy, on the contrary, never bases itself on the data of history, mathematics or physics, nor on any other presuppositions, but is really a "science based on an ultimate foundation."[12]

Scientific "Objectivity"

A final characteristic of contemporary science can perhaps be seen in the fact that the sciences make be-ing appear only in that kind of "objectivity" which is constituted and maintained by the various scientific objectivations.[13] This point needs to be explained somewhat more in detail. At the same time, we will have an oppor-

---

[11]*Ibid.,* pp. 49, 56-58.
[12]*Ibid.,* p. 90.
[13]*Ibid.,* pp. 155-156.

tunity to throw some additional light on the preceding three "assertions" about the essence of science and to show that they are well-founded.

As we have already seen, the primordial root and source of meaning is not found in a relationship of knowing but in a relationship of being. Knowing is only a special way of our being-in-the-world. The characteristic feature of this way of being-in-the-world is that man confines himself to "looking at" the world without being totally involved in it.

This contemplative "looking at" always implies a particular attitude of man toward the be-ings in the world; hence the things that are encountered in this way are always seen from a particular viewpoint. Which aspect these be-ings will reveal to the "theoretical man" depends on his attitude with regard to them. By making that aspect the object of a critical and methodical inquiry, the theoretical man lays the foundation for a particular science.

Accordingly, by his very attitude toward the things that are there, the man of science defines an area of the intraworldly sphere as the domain of his object. The discovery and the precise delimitation of a well-defined domain seems to be the first step of every scientific research. The assertion that the "object" of each of the sciences represents a well-defined domain is evident from the fact that the "object" prescribes *a priori* the way in which possible problems should arise. Every new phenomenon emerging in such a domain is examined as long as it fits into the normative object totality of the science in question.[14] The problem now is how this discovery and this delimitation of such an object domain take place.

Thematization

Heidegger thinks that in every theoretical, and *a fortiori* in every scientific orientation toward the world, the scien-

---

[14]*Holzwege,* pp. 56-58.

tific experience itself contains already a special thematization in which the object of knowledge is taken, constituted and projected as its theme.[15]   In this projecting, a certain domain of be-ings is staked out, the approach to this domain is given its particular methodic direction, the structure of the conceptual and discursive explanation receives its orientation, and a specific "language" is constituted.

The thematization comprises the above-mentioned primordial project, the staking out of a definite object domain, the determination of the method as the approach to this domain, and the orientation of the conceptual structure and of the linguistic expressions proper to this domain.   The purpose of thematization is to free a worldly be-ing or a particular group of be-ings in such a way that they can become the object of purely theoretical discovery and therefore can be examined "objectively."

Heidegger, then, demands that every science be "objective," that it adhere to the facts; but he refuses to admit that these facts can be *completely* "dehumanized" (scientism) or ought to be *completely* divorced from the world (idealism).   The reason for his refusal is that the scientific subject also is a being-in-the-world and as such continues to be at least partially involved in it.[16]

To clarify his position, Heidegger distinguishes between the "being available as equipment" of the worldly be-ings in our everyday concernful dealing and their "merely being present at hand" when we assume the scientific attitude. He argues that just as our daily concern precedes our scientific "looking at," so also "being available as equipment" precedes "merely being present at hand."   Before we are able to conceive something under a special aspect in a limiting and abstracting consideration, we must already have been confronted with this thing in its fullness in an all-embracing relation in which we were totally involved.

---

[15] *S.Z.*, p. 363.
[16] *S.Z.*, pp. 59-62, 363.

Accordingly, the shift in standpoint of the theoretical man has an abstracting and limiting function, by virtue of which that which is primordially given is broken up in such a way that one aspect can be sharply illuminated. Thus every science, even in its scientific experience, is rooted in the *a priori* character of the formal aspect under which a thing is considered.

Everything else depends on this formal aspect: the foundations of scientific research, the method, the "language," the type of argumentation, the mode of intelligibility, and the conception of truth and certitude. Thus, at the root of every science we find a "making present" of a worldly be-ing. This "making present" differs from our everyday concern, it aims solely at disclosing be-ings in an "objective" way, i.e., as pure data of theoretical observation, as "merely being there."[17]

The Scientific Object is Something Abstract

The ultimate material object of a science is the perceived real. The task of science is to describe that which is perceived as "merely present at hand," i.e., from the viewpoint of ontic objectivation. Thus it follows that science is not only abstract in itself but that its proper object also must always be something abstract. For reality as "merely there" is only the correlate of a secondary intentionality which has its foundation in, and results from, our primordial intention, our existence itself. If, then, in science we speak of reality as an object by itself, we envisage it from the start according to a dimension which is only virtually contained in perception, but with which it does not coincide completely.

In comparison to perceived reality, objective reality is an explanation but at the same time also an impoverishment. Science makes an objective aspect of the primordial perception explicit, but in doing so it turns away from the real be-ing in the full sense of the term, in order to dis-

[17]*S.Z.*, pp. 153-160; 356-364.

cover and explain one of its aspects. Since this aspect is indeed an aspect of the real, science remains knowledge of reality. Accordingly, the explicitation and explanation of the purely objective side of the real leads to a specific meaning which truly belongs to that be-ing, but only from the viewpoint of its "merely being present at hand." This meaning can be disclosed only by a method and by cognitive processes that correspond to the proper object.

CHAPTER TEN

REFLECTIONS ON LANGUAGE AND TERMINOLOGY

1. Peculiarities of Heidegger's Language

Starting with *Being and Time,* Heidegger's works are written in a peculiar language. This language appears not only occasionally, but permeates his work through and through, although it is not without modifications. Heidegger's language covers a vast range, but we will limit ourselves to a brief consideration of the philosophical terms which he uses especially in his description of the mode of being proper to man.

Two Groups of Terms

We can distinguish at once two large groups of such technical terms and expressions. On the one hand, we find a certain number of Latin words or words derived from Latin. These generally refer to the formal aspect of his studies and emphasize their strictly theoretical character. To this group belong terms as "structure," "mode," "modality," "character," "constitutive," and "deficient." On the other hand, there are many words which either belong to or have been derived from ordinary German but which are not likely to be encountered as technical terms in a philosophical study. To this group belong such words as care (*Sorge*), *Dasein,* equipment (*Zeug*), involvement (*Bewandtniss*), "moodness" (*Befindlichkeit*), project (*Entwurf*), conscience (*Gewissen*), and to temporalize (*zeitigen*). Moreover, Heidegger, quite frequently constructs rather complex German phrases in order to express with accuracy the basic existential characteristic of *Dasein.*

The crucial term of his whole reflection on man, the word "existence," does not quite harmonize with this division, since it belongs to the formalizing terminology that is typical of scholasticism. However, so far as its content is concerned, "existence" represents the key term outlining the entire horizon of his anthropological conceptualization. Anyhow, the contrast between the abstract character of the first group of words and the closeness to real life of the second group gives a special character to Heidegger's work. Yet one cannot say that this contrast makes his work ambiguous.

Traditional Terms

In his use of the traditional terms of philosophy one can clearly observe that Heidegger uses them with a certain freedom. When it suits him, he derives a new word from a traditional term; such practice, however, is not unusual in German. Thus he speaks of "existent*ial*" and "existent*iel*"; and, in addition to the adjectival "existiential," he also uses the noun "existentiale" to denote the essential structural aspects of *Dasein's* being as being-in-the-world. He also speaks of "ontic" in opposition to "ontological."

Moreover, it happens frequently that a standard term receives an entirely new meaning; as for instance "existence." In such cases Heidegger remains generally truthful to the way the word has been formed; for example, he describes "existence" as "standing out toward," "standing open for," "stepping out to" since "existence" can be taken as "ex-sistence." In his later works Heidegger likes to write it "ec-sistence." This attention to points suggested by original parts of a word manifests itself likewise in the hyphenation of the word "ec-stasis." Such splitting of words into syllables often increases the plasticity of expressions.

German Words

The living vernacular offers even greater opportunities for such procedures and Heidegger takes full advantage of them. Boldly, but nevertheless cautiously, he let himself be guided by the genius of the German language. First of all, it is striking that he avoids as much as possible the customary technical terms. Such words as "soul," "spirit," "consciousness," "subject," and "object" are but sparingly used in his works, and even then mostly in connection with the views of other philosophers.

Heidegger sometimes attributes two different meanings to words which are synonymous in ordinary parlance. For instance, he opposes dread to fear and then paraphrases both in a way which does not completely coincide with their generally accepted meaning.

Through prefixes and suffixes, Heidegger enlarges his carefully chosen vocabulary with refined differentiations. In the process he creates new German words, which, however, conform to the rules governing analogous cases.

At times obsolete or forgotten terms are reintroduced, as, for instance, *Befindlichkeit,* which was still used in the seventeenth century and which we have translated as "moodness." Sometimes variations of a basic word appear together in one and the same context to accentuate the common root; for instance, he speaks of *das sich überhörende Hinhören,* "the listening [away from one's own self to the 'they'] that fails to hear."

Occasionally he also assigns new meanings to existing words. The German term *zeitigen* means "to mature" or "to bring to maturity," but Heidegger makes it mean "to temporalize," to create the structures of time. In this way he gives the word a much more profound meaning than is usual in ordinary speech and draws attention to something that may or must have been at the basis of the accepted meaning. A typlical example of such a linguistic creation which follows the rules of word derivation and yet leads to a completely new word with a totally new meaning is *Entfernung.* This word is composed of the privative prefix *ent-,* the stem *fern* (far), and the ending *-ung,* making it a noun. Heidegger uses it in the sense of "removing distance," bringing close.

Heidegger not only forges new words through combinations but he sometimes also detaches a component from accepted combinations; for instance, he gives the word *Zeug* the meaning of equipment which by itself it hardly ever has, though it can mean this in a compound.

Heidegger, however, rarely violates the grammar of the German language in these renewals and changes. When he does so—for instance, in creating the *present* participle *gewesende,* "in the process of having been," from the *past* participle *gewesen,* "having been"—he apologizes for taking such liberties and tries to indicate why they are unavoidable.

These remarks, of course, do not exhaust all the linguistic peculiarities of Heidegger's work. One would have to consider also the dialectical features that occasionally are found in his language and the strange way in which he often constructs his sentences. The above mentioned examples of Heideggerian linguistics, which we have borrowed from J. Aler,[1] are offered only as specimens of his attitude toward language.

2. JUSTIFICATION OF HEIDEGGER'S LANGUAGE

Phenomenological Reduction to the "Lived World"

We must now ask ourselves why Heidegger assumed this attitude. In attempting to answer this question, one should keep in mind that Heidegger's ultimate aim is to build a new ontology and that he considers an analytics of man's being a necessary condition for this work. The method he follows in this analytics is phenomenology, which permits him to adopt the usual philosophical terminology in the formal part of his work. On the other hand, as far as the content of the analysis is concerned, the

---

[1] "De taal bij Heidegger," *Alg. Ned. Tijdschrift v. Wetenschap en Psychologie,* vol LIII (1961), pp. 241-260.

phenomena have to be described according to the demands of phenomenology, that is, as they manifest themselves immediately and, therefore, as they are in themselves.

Man, however, has opinions about almost everything, including himself. These have been developed during the course of many centuries, and greatly influenced by traditional philosophy and the sciences. Heidegger's analysis of man's being is not concerned with the opinions one has about things and man, but with letting things and man appear primordially as they are. We are used to expressing the accepted views in a commonly accepted language. This language does not always express that which *is,* but what is thought about it. If, then, one wants to describe unambiguously that which appears primordially as it is in itself, one is practically forced to develop a new terminology.

Thus Heidegger's linguistic peculiarities can be explained, at least in part, by the fact that it is necessary to reduce the cultural world phenomenologically to the "lived world." Wherever Heidegger finds himself compelled to avoid the accepted words and technical terms and forced to find or create new possibilities of expressions, he always tries to adhere as much as possible to rules of the German idiom or to the procedures which are used in analogous cases elsewhere. Very often also he searches in the history of the language for obsolete and forgotten words which can express that which shows itself immediately in the analysis.

The Example of "Aletheia"

On other occasions he attempts to endow existing words with a more primordial meaning by going back to Greek or sometimes to Latin. The reason is that the old Greek philosophers were less influenced by culture and therefore must have been much closer to the primordial phenomena than we are. For instance, he conceives *aletheia* etymologically as un-concealedness (*a-letheia*) and uses this etymology to confirm his own interpretation of what truth existentially is, namely, "to be dis-covering." Although he does not claim that the Greeks ever understood it this way, his interpretation of the term appears to be supported by his phenomenological analysis of truth. His explanation of *aletheia* clarifies the content of this term and can be defended, especially if one can explain how this conception of truth had to lead of necessity to its generally accepted interpretation.[2] Whether the Greeks ever intended it or not, one can say that etymologically the word points in this direction and this is precisely the point which Heidegger considers important.

3. Heidegger's Philosophy of Language in "Being and Time"

Preliminary Remarks

After what has been said above it will not be surprising that in his view of *Dasein's* own being Heidegger attributes a very special place to language and places particular emphasis on the word. As we have said, Heidegger writes an analysis of *Dasein* in order to use it as the foundation of a general theory of being. This preparatory reflection has two phases. First, certain structures of man's being are described as an introduction, and then these structures are thoroughly explained as modes of primordial temporality. The essence of man reveals itself clearly only in temporality and, in turn, time forms the horizon for man's understanding of being.

As can be expected, in the introductory part of his analytics Heidegger discusses the phenomenon of language. He wants to account for the question of who really is the be-ing that in its being has already entered into a relationship to its own being. He sees the essence of this being in existence. Two aspects are included in the fundamental openness of existence:

1. I am, I know that I am, I am conscious that I am thrown into being and always find myself in it already.

---

[2] *S.Z.*, p. 220.

2. On the other hand, existence also means that what I will make of my being is left up to me. In other words, I also experience myself as a project in which, always anticipating objectives and from there returning to the means that are necessary to attain them, I nevertheless cannot escape my original "being thrown."

In its project *Dasein* can be in an authentic or in an inauthentic mode. Both modes must be considered carefully. The same is true of the existentialia which are in both cases common to *Dasein* because they are necessarily connected with the openness of *Dasein's* own being.

The phenomenon of language is raised rather late in these reflections, viz., only in the second last chapter of the introductory analysis. What Heidegger says there about language is at first disappointing. One would expect that he would extensively elaborate on this eminently fundamental anthropological phenomenon. Heidegger, however, takes the same attitude toward the phenomenon of language as he does toward most other "fundamental forms" of being-man, such as consciousness, freedom, theoretical knowledge, and experience. Heidegger looks precisely for something even more profound, namely, the primary mode of being-man as the ontic-ontological condition of these "fundamental forms" of man's being. He thinks that this primary mode cannot be reached through these fundamental forms, but that it can be done in terms of the phenomenological characterization of *Dasein* as being-in-the-world.

An Apparent Contradiction

Moreover, there seems to be a contradiction in Heidegger's reflections on language. On the one hand, he asserts several times[3] that language appears as an ontological derivative of reason, but on the other, the analysis of the structure of disclosedness shows that language already comes to light in the advanced analysis of primordial

---

[3]*S.Z.*, pp. 130 ff. and 160 ff.

understanding. We must therefore try to explain this apparent contradiction.

Expression and Language

Heidegger begins to discuss language as soon as he undertakes analyzing primordial understanding. As we have seen, he describes primordial understanding as an interpreting apprehension in which *Dasein* discovers itself as power to be. But this interpreting constitution of meaning as such is not yet expressed and explicit. It can be explained in its different aspects through an explicitation (*Auslegung*), in which the meaning of things is really discovered. This primordial explicitation finally can be expressed explicitly in and through assertion (*Aussage*). Expression, however, does not necessarily have to be verbal but encompasses everything in which *Dasein* can make its explicitated understanding known.

Heidegger distinguishes three aspects in this expression of understanding, viz., pointing out, predicating and communicating; but language is discussed only in the last of these aspects. Communication is, according to Heidegger, a mode of pointing out and predicating. In connection with this it should be noted that predicating is not yet thought of in terms of language. On the other hand, in predicating, the transition from being occupied with something to speaking with others about something takes place already. Such a restriction, however, presupposes the pointing out of a "this here" about which one wants to speak. From this pointing out the elements of predicating, the subject and predicate, arise.[4]

Explicitation and Communication

On the other hand, pointing out for further characterization presupposes a meaning which one wants to assign formally in a judgment to what is being pointed out.

[4] *S.Z.*, pp. 154-155.

It must already have been known that it is possible for what is being pointed out to have this meaning. It is the task of the explicitation to show that it can have this meaning. Thus, Heidegger bases the phenomenon of language on what he calls "communication" and communication itself on explicitation.

Thus the explicitation makes us penetrate to greater depth in our derivation of language from the openness of existence. For in this explicitation one unfolds the meaning which in circumspective concern belongs to something. This unfolding comes about in concern itself. If, for example, someone repairs a piece of broken equipment, he "stands still" by it. In that case the equipment draws attention to itself and its meaning is expressly delineated. Usually, however, one moves about in the routine network of mutual relations, in which used things refer to one another and thus receive and give meanings to one another.

Yet, the functional totality of references always point beyond the equipment toward man as their ultimate "what . . . for." Equipment serves man and forms the field of man's possibilities. Man does not find these possibilities nor does he read them anywhere, but he dis-covers them. His project, his meaning-giving action, constitutes the referential totality of equipment in which the things reveal themselves to *Dasein* according to their meaning. The explicitation develops the possibilities projected by primordial understanding and unfolds the meanings that were already established. This referential totality itself, that was already structured prior to any explicitating interpretation, this multi-unity of possible significations, arises primarily through primordial understanding. Only at this point does Heidegger attain the ontological foundation for language in a fundamental structure of existence itself.

We have gone through this long series again in reversed order to make abundantly clear where, according to

Heidegger, language should come to light in the analytics of *Dasein* and how the phenomenon of language is founded on primordial understanding.

Language and Reason

Despite the fact that Heidegger speaks about language in his analysis of primordial understanding, he expressly states that language is a derivative of the third existentiale of *Dasein's* openness, namely, logos or discursive reasoning. In the context of analytics this is a deliberate consequence of the phenomenological method and not at all a faulty explanation that later has to be set straight. The description distinguishes each time a plurality of characteristics which are correlated, equivalent and mutually determining. Thus the unity of the structure as a totality can clearly be preserved in spite of the analysis. *Dasein's* openness is constituted by its fundamental "mood," primordial understanding and reason. Heidegger discusses these three one by one in this sequence, but also always understands them through and in terms of one another. The fundamental "mood" is already understanding, and understanding is always in a certain "mood." He discusses these two constituents also in their reciprocal implication with regard to the third (reason). Yet reason sometimes appears to take a secondary place, in spite of the fact that it is said to be equiprimordial with the fundamental "mood" and primordial understanding.

Accordingly, in the series of existentialia which start from understanding and go to assertion, the activity of reason is already included. In this way the above-mentioned apparent contradiction disappears.

Inauthentic Speech

It is also very striking that, in developing his view of authentic and inauthentic being, Heidegger speaks about the phenomenon of language mostly in connection with inauthentic being. When *Being and Time* more amply discusses language, Heidegger depicts especially idle talk of *Dasein* in its fallen state. The same happens when he mentions language in connection with care and with temporality.[5] In a negative way the same happens again when, in connection with conscience, he argues that reason in authentic being is wordless.[6] Accordingly, in Heidegger's eyes, speech is generally peculiar to *Dasein* in its fallen state, and only thinkers and poets can undo its degeneration.[7]

---

[5]*S.Z.*, pp. 167 ff., 212 ff., 335 ff.
[6]*S.Z.*, pp. 270 ff.
[7]For Heidegger's later philosophy of language, see *Unterwegs zur Sprache,* Pfullingen, 1959.

CHAPTER ELEVEN

THE QUESTION OF THE MEANING OF BEING

As we have mentioned several times, Heidegger's existential analyses of human *Dasein* should be understood in an ontological perspective, that is, as a preparation for a concrete development of the question about the meaning of Being. If one separates his analyses from this ultimate aim, one does not understand them as intended by Heidegger. In his philosophical work he wants to disclose the foundations which are needed to explain what Being really is.

Heidegger thinks that he can discover the ground for this fundamental understanding in an analysis of *Dasein's* own being, insofar as *Dasein* is the be-ing in which the understanding of Being appears and is constantly again reenacted. In this sense existential analysis is already a fundamental ontology.[1] In his analyses of *Dasein* Heidegger does not intend to give us a kind of psychoanalysis or defend a new form of subjectivism. He is not concerned with factualities; on the contrary, his ultimate aim is to make Being itself evident by bringing to light the roots of the understanding of Being.

Heidegger was not able to realize this aim in *Being and Time*. The results to which the existential analytics contained in *Being and Time* lead even appear to exclude any positive viewpoint in regard to Being itself; consequently, they also seem to make ontology, in the accepted sense of the word, impossible. This seems to be the reason why the last part of *Being and Time* has never appeared, and probably will never be published. In his later writings, however, Heidegger constantly returns to the question of the meaning of Being. He now thinks to have found a

---

[1] *S.Z.*, p. 13.

way through which one could come to a positive solution of this question without having to give up the results of his existential analytics, although these results often receive a different interpretation in terms of his later acquired insight.

In the present chapter we would like to develop and clarify these points. The most suitable starting point seems to lie in a survey of the most important descriptions of *Dasein's* essence.

1. EXISTENCE AS THE ESSENCE OF DASEIN

In *Being and Time* Heidegger says that "the essence of *Dasein* lies in its existence."[2] Let us clarify what he means through an example. By saying of a table that it is, one wants to express that once it is made, it is definitively determined in its being. Of itself, the table cannot change and has no possibility to relate itself either toward itself or toward other be-ings. There are no possibilities at all for it. For man, however, the situation is entirely different. In his being man is not determined once and for all. His being is distinguished from that of things precisely in that it can always be further realized. By seizing his given possibilities freely in a certain way, he arrives at the way of being proper to him.

These possibilities are not purely logical possibilities, but in a certain sense they constitute that which is most real in man. For man always and of necessity relates himself to these possibilities, we may even say that he *is* these possibilities. "That be-ing for which in its being this very being is at stake, relates itself toward its being as its ownmost possibility."[3] Insofar as *Dasein* always *is* its possibilities, it is constantly also already more than it is now. This "already being more" is a "being ahead of itself." Insofar as man always transcends himself, insofar as he is "with" his possibilities, man exists.

[2] *S.Z.,* p. 42.
[3] *S.Z.,* p. 42.

Thus man himself determines his own being; any activity of *Dasein* is always a self-determination already, so that at each moment it is also responsible for its own being. Because of this fundamental power to be, *Dasein's* being is always a task: "The 'essence' (*Wesen*) of this be-ing lies in its 'to be' (*Zu-sein*)."[4] We must add that the being of each *Dasein* is characterized by "mine-ness" (*Jemeinigkeit*); that is, each man's own being is proper to him alone, it is given to him as his possibility, as his task: "The being which is at stake for this be-ing in its being is in each case mine."[5]

Dasein's Structural Element of Mood

To exist therefore means that *Dasein* relates itself to its own being as power to be. What this implies is best explained in terms of the fundamental mood and primordial understanding. In the fundamental mood man's being--in-the-world is disclosed in a primordial way. As Heidegger says, "The attunement of 'moodness' existentially constitutes *Dasein's* openness to the world."[6] It is characteristic of man that what he encounters immediately appeals to him in such a way that it puts him in a certain fundamental mood, such as joy, pleasure, contentment, or fear.

In and through this mood it is already clear to man how what he encounters belongs to him and what attitude he must assume toward it. At the same time, and this is of special importance, man discovers his own way of being in this fundamental mood. Thus, the primary function of mood is that it enlightens man about his own way of being and that it simultaneously discloses be-ings in their relation to *Dasein*. In and through the fundamental mood *Dasein* is disclosed to itself and at the same time be-ings are discovered.

---

[4]*S.Z.*, p. 42.
[5]*S.Z.*, p. 42.
[6]*S.Z.*, p. 137.

Dasein's Structural Element of Understanding

The second essential aspect of *Dasein's* structure is primordial understanding. Just as man, as soon as he is, is in a certain mood, so likewise does he at once display a certain form of understanding. Mood and understanding are equiprimordial and are always encountered together. Heidegger defines primordial understanding in terms of man's project. This project has nothing to do with a preconceived plan, but refers to *Dasein's* self-projection toward its possibilities in which *Dasein* discovers at the same time the encountered be-ings. In the project *Dasein* makes room for its own possibilities, and at the same time it constitutes the world as the referential totality on which it always depends.[7]

In its understanding project *Dasein* throws light upon the world and the intraworldly be-ings as well as its own being. Accordingly, by characterizing *Dasein* as primordial understanding, Heidegger wants to express that man is the be-ing that in itself is primordially light. In other words, *Dasein* is the be-ing that understands itself and that also throws light on and "unconceals" other beings, i.e., it is a be-ing that can experience be-ings as be-ings. For this reason *Dasein* occupies a very special place among the be-ings insofar as it is the only be-ing that can relate itself to itself and to other be-ings. This relating always assumes a different structure according as the be-ing to which *Dasein* relates itself belongs to a different domain of be-ings, viz., *Dasein's* own being, "being with," being "ready to hand" and "merely being present at hand." This point has already been discussed sufficiently in the preceding chapters.

Dasein and "Letting Be"

Thus we see that even in *Being and Time* openness is clearly described as a fundamental characteristic of *Dasein's* own being. In his later works Heidegger in-

[7] *S.Z.,* p. 145.

creasingly emphasizes this openness. Further reflection upon what he says there about openness leads us to a second group of descriptions of *Dasein's* essence. By stating that *Dasein* is essentially openness, Heidegger wants to say that it is proper to *Dasein* that be-ings can encounter *Dasein* in what they are and as they are. *Dasein's* openness is the necessary condition for the possibility of being "at" (*bei*) be-ings.

The proper activity of *Dasein's* being "at," however, is not work, i.e., making be-ings become different. For making be-ings be different always presupposes as a necessary condition that *Dasein* can make the other be-ings come to itself as they are in themselves. This is what Heidegger calls "letting be." "Letting be" does not have the negative meaning of "let it be, I do not worry about it any more," but positively means "to have something to do with it." Nevertheless, although the be-ings in question are not changed, something happens in letting them be: an openness is disclosed in which the be-ings that become disclosed can appear as they are. "Having something to do with the unconcealment of a be-ing does not stop there [at the unconcealing], but develops into a withdrawal before this be-ing so that it may reveal itself as what it is and how it is. . . . As 'letting be' it 'exposes' itself to that be-ing-as-it-is and brings all its relations to it into the open. 'Letting be' . . . is in itself 'ex-posing,' 'ex-sistent,' . . . the 'ex-position' of be-ings into unconcealedness."[8]

Dasein's Openness

If one wants to reflect upon the essence of *Dasein,* one has to try to think about the history of this "giving of openness." If, however, to "letting be" there belongs essentially a domain of unconcealedness which is opened by "letting be" itself; and if "letting be" is essential to

---

[8]*Vom Wesen der Wahrheit,* p. 15.

Dasein; then there exists a new possibility to describe *Dasein's* own being. *Dasein* then becomes "placing one-self in the sphere of openness." Because this sphere is precisely that in which be-ings begin to appear and are taken from concealedness, one can say that "Ex-sistence is the 'ex-position' of be-ings into unconcealedness." The expression "the 'essence' of *Dasein* lies in its existence," then, means that *Dasein* is that be-ing to which it is proper to "make room" for other be-ings so that they can show themselves as they are. According to Heidegger, a domain of disclosedness opens itself immediately as soon as *Dasein* is, so that be-ings are able to meet *Dasein* in this sphere of openness. The essence of *Dasein's* being is to open up room in which be-ings can become manifest to *Dasein.*[9]

---

[9]*Ibid.,* pp. 10-17.

2. The Reason for Dasein's Privileged Position Among be-ings

A very fundamental problem remains to be considered: How is it possible that *Dasein* can play this role among the other be-ings? According to Heidegger, this possibility is connected with man's relation to Being. To understand the relation between *Dasein* and Being, one must first consider the question of the relation between be-ing and Being.

Traditional Metaphysics

The Greeks used the word "be-ing" (*to on*) to indicate everything that is: men, houses, stones, trees, dogs, God. All of them in one way or another are be-ings. To dis-tinguish between God and the other be-ings philosophers later spoke about an "infinite be-ing" (*ens infinitum*) in opposition to finite be-ings, although, of course, there is only one infinite be-ing. The exact meaning of "being," however, usually remained unexplained. According to Heidegger, the great mistake of classical metaphysics was that it tried to speak about be-ings in a definitive way without paying attention to being itself. Anyhow, traditional metaphysics considered be-ing as be-ing; it tried to throw light on the proper character of be-ing by defining it as physis, energy, matter, spirit, will, subject, etc.

But, one will object, is being itself not included in these descriptions of traditional metaphysics? Heidegger does not think so, for the attention remained directed to the be-ings themselves, to their "be-ingness," and not to Being itself. One could insist that traditional metaphysics does not want to limit itself to be-ings since it really wants to transcend be-ings; for example, when it asks about the ultimate cause of be-ings. Heidegger admits that traditional metaphysics wants to transcend be-ings, but argues that its search for the ultimate cause does not go beyond the domain of be-ings. The highest be-ing as cause (*Ursache*) is still regarded as a thing (*Ur-sache*). Moreover, traditional metaphysics tried to understand the relation between the highest be-ing and the other be-ings by way of analogy with the relations between finite be-ings.

Spaciousness and Being

Thus, metaphysics understands the domain of be-ing, but not yet the domain of be-ings *as such* in its "spaciousness" (*Geräumigkeit*). By "spaciousness" Heidegger means that which primordially creates and gives room. The "open space" which results from it gives be-ings the possibility to appear insofar as this space makes room for them. This "open space" is experienced by man as unconcealedness, as *a-letheia,* truth. In this perspective truth is the proper dwelling place of *Dasein.* "Spaciousness," which causes this "open space," cannot be a be-ing, but is Being itself.

In truth, as primordial unconcealedness, Being gives itself; it guides itself, so to speak, to *Dasein.* But this self-giving is at the same time a self-concealing. By conceiving Being as "spaciousness" which, as it were, makes room for itself in the open space it creates, one tries, according to Heidegger, to conceive the fundamental characteristic of Being. This characteristic could also be indicated by the term "clearing" (*Lichtung*), an expression which can mean both an open space in the woods and a giving of light. Only because man has his dwelling in the "spaciousness" and the "clearing" of Being, and only because Being itself is thereby a giver of light and of "space," is man able to know and relate himself to the be-ing that thereby has become disclosed.[10]

"Standing out Toward" the Truth of Being

In this perspective one arrives at a third description of *Dasein's* existence. In his *Letter on Humanism* Heidegger writes: " 'Ex-sistence' means, so far as its content is concerned, 'to stand out toward' the truth of Being."[11] This means that *Dasein* is the only be-ing whose essence has to be defined through a relation to Being itself and this in such a way that this relation means a being open to the openness of Being. To "ex-sist" and to transcend oneself mean to "stand out toward," but no longer primarily in the sense of "transcending oneself" or of "being ahead of one's possibilities," but in the sense of standing in the openness which the truth of Being is.[12]

Hence *Dasein* is man's openness to the fundamental openness of Being itself. *Dasein* is certainly a light and illuminating, but only insofar as it is made to give light by Being which is essentially lighting. "Man is not the lord of be-ings. Man is the shepherd of Being. . . . Man is the neighbor of Being."[13] In *Being and Time, Dasein* was mentioned as "lighting" and "illuminating" without any reference to Being. "To say that [*Dasein*] is 'illumi-

---

[10]Cf. *Was ist Metaphysik?*, pp. 19-23; *Brief über den Humanismus*, pp. 82-83; *Platons Lehre van der Wahrheit*, p. 48.

[11]*Brief über den Humanismus*, p. 70.

[12]*Ibid.*, pp. 66-67, 91; *Was ist Metaphysik?*, pp. 14-15.

[13]*Brief über den Humanismus*, p. 90.

nated' means that *as* being-in-the-world it is 'lighted' (*gelichtet*) in itself, not through any other be-ing, but in such a way that it *is* itself 'lighting.' "[14]

Because man has this unique relation to Being, be-ings can meet him; he can place them before himself, and be conscious of them. "All consciousness presupposes the 'ec-statically' conceived existence as the 'essence' of man. 'Essence' here means that which man is insofar as he is man."[15] The definition of man as *Dasein,* as "ex-sistence," is of necessity presupposed by any possible relationship to be-ing. Concepts of any such relationship always imply the primordial ground of man's being. His being is presupposed in one way or another in all other definitions of man's essence, although this ground does not have to be thematically present in them.

Harmonious Development

The development of Heidegger's thinking which we have tried to indicate here does not consist in the correction of a previously held view. On the contrary, in his later statements his earlier ideas are maintained, although they often function in a different context. Heidegger seems to speak on different levels; he always penetrates more profoundly, but in his progress there is but rarely need to refer to prior findings as incorrect. What at first presented itself in this or that way, appears to be different after further reflection. For ontology is concerned with matters that at first do not yet show themselves within the matters that present themselves immediately and as such. That which conceals itself has to be brought to light laboriously. This cannot be done immediately, but goes through many phases. Although these phases bring to light data that differ from one another, these data are not necessarily contradictory.

---

[14]*S.Z.,* p. 133.
[15]*Was ist Metaphysik?,* p. 16.

In any case, it appears evident that, with due regard for his later writings, Heidegger can hardly be called an atheist, a nihilist, a subjectivist, a pessimist or an idealist. From his later writings it is clear that for him Being is not a project of man and that in his perspective the giving of meaning has only a limited range. Man's "project is essentially a 'thrown' project. That which 'is throwing' in the 'projecting' is not man but Being itself, which sends man into the 'ex-sistence' of *Dasein* as its essence."[16]

3. Dread and "No-thing"

A similar conclusion is reached when one examines what Heidegger says in his different works about the fundamental concepts "dread" and "no-thing." In *Being and Time* the concept "no-thing" or "non-be-ing" occupies only a very small place and there appears to be no question yet that "no-thing" can open a perspective on Being itself. In his later works the concept "no-thing" comes more frequently to the fore and is finally even identified with Being. To clarify what Heidegger writes in his later works, we must first return to his viewpoint in *Being and Time*. A few brief repetitions will be unavoidable. Let us first, however, indicate what the problem of "dread" and "no-thing" is.

The Importance of Dread and "No-thing"

According to Heidegger, the notions of dread and "no-thing" are so closely connected that one cannot speak of the one without paying attention to the other. Yet in their unsolved correlation, "no-thing" has a certain priority. The primorial datum to which both concepts refer is, according to Heidegger, not a concrete experience alongside all other possible experiences. When all the structures which at first present themselves to *Dasein's* analytic gaze have been made explicit, they reveal themselves to be ulti-

---

[16] *Brief über den Humanismus,* p. 84.

mately derivative structures. Thus the problem is to discover the mode of being in which *Dasein* manifests itself primordially and totally. For probably only in this mode of being can one find a track leading to the final aim of the analysis, viz., to understand the meaning of being and to understand *Dasein's* own being in the light of Being.

In *Being and Time* Heidegger lays emphasis on this line of thought, for he speaks about reality and truth immediately after care.[17] Whatever one may think about Heidegger's analysis of care, it shows in any case that one can understand what being is only after disclosing the essence of the be-ing that understands be-ings, itself, and being; and this be-ing is precisely man. Only then can one hope to clarify the mystery of understanding being which is present in *Dasein* and to go on to the even more fundamental mystery contained in Being itself which enters into relationship with *Dasein* in and through the understanding of being. In *Being and Time* Heidegger approaches these problems in terms of dread. In his later works he connects them more closely with the concept of "no-thing." However, even in *Being and Time* "no-thing" plays already a role, as is evidenced by the following paragraph.

Dasein's Dread of "No-thing"

What becomes manifest in dread? In reading Heidegger's answer to this question, one has to keep in mind that he wants to describe only that which shows itself, in the way it shows itself: "To let that which shows itself be seen from itself exactly as it shows itself from itself."[18] In other words, he wants to describe it without any theory which one could develop with data beyond the immediately given phenomenon. Heidegger's answer to the question is as follows: "That which [*Dasein*] dreads is not an intraworldly be-ing. Thus it is essentially incapable of having

---

[17]*S.Z.*, pp. 180 ff, 200 ff, 219 ff.
[18]*S.Z.*, p. 34.

an involvement with it."[19] What, then, causes *Dasein's* dread? "In that which [*Dasein*] dreads, the 'It is no-thing and nowhere' becomes manifest."[20] But this "no-thing 'ready to hand' . . . is not totally no-thing. The 'no-thing' of 'readiness to hand' is grounded in the most primordial 'something,' in the world. . . . Hence, if the 'no-thing,' that is, the world as such, exhibits itself as that which [*Dasein*] dreads, this means that being-in-the-world itself is that which dread dreads."[21]

These texts could perhaps be clarified as follows. With the expression being-in-the-world Heidegger wants to indicate that we always already stand in relation to "something." We always experience ourselves in such a relation, and we experience ourselves also only if we realize this fundamental relation; in a certain sense we even *are* this fundamental relation. In all my actions I am intentionally related to something: my knowing, my loving, my valuing, my willing always imply an intentional relationship. Insofar as we realize our own being, we are in a primordial relation to a horizon of possible things. At first it seems that all forms of our relating to being become concrete and precise in the things in which we are actually involved within this horizon. Heidegger, however, wants to show that all forms of concernfully dealing with intraworldly be-ings derive their source from a dimension which nearly always remains hidden but which shows itself in dread in a primordial way. In dread something manifests itself that is totally different from what manifests itself in the totality of relations to intrawordly be-ings. Contrary to what happens in fear, which is always related to an intrawordly be-ing, in dread *everything* loses its meaning immediately. What I am in dread cannot possibly be understood by relating myself to an intrawordly be-ing. That which I dread is "no-thing" and nothing can help me here.

---

[19] *S.Z.*, p. 186.
[20] *S.Z.*, p. 186.
[21] *S.Z.*, p. 187.

Yet I am and remain "in relation to . . . ," but that to which I am related in dread is not an intrawordly thing, not a be-ing to which I am able to relate myself. All these be-ings have lost their meaning here. In dread I appear only as a pure "relation to . . . ," and these dots can never be replaced by any be-ing whatsoever. In dread, therefore, *Dasein* experiences itself in its own being as pure "relation to . . . ," but that to which I am related cannot at all be an intrawordly be-ing. In dread it becomes clear to me what it really means to be "in relation to. . . ." Accordingly, the expression "being-in-the-world" does not mean any longer a relation to a intrawordly be-ing as I might suspect in my everyday attitude, but it means only the fundamental structure of the pure "relation to . . . ," which cannot further be explicitated by any be-ing.

The "No-thing" is Real

The "no-thing," however, that manifests itself as a *phenomenon* in dread is, as "no-thing of intrawordly be-ings," no less real than these be-ings. In a certain sense it is even more real insofar as this "no-thing" does not originate from an enumeration of the intrawordly be-ings and insofar as every intrawordly be-ing loses its meaning in the presence of the "no-thing." We face here a problem that must be approached from the usual dimension of our everyday life in a negative manner.

In this fundamental negativity Heidegger sees the root of all other forms of negativity, yet there is no question here of pure negativity. There is "something" here that manifests itself positively, that rises above everything else and brings it to silence. Yet one cannot define it as pure nothingness, and every positive expression makes the phenomenon that discloses itself in dread confused and misrepresents it. The positive content of what manifests itself in the phenomenon of dread can come to light in a primordial way only to one who dares to enter into this experience. Even then it cannot yet be expressed in words, even then it still covers everything with its shadow.

Dasein as Pure "Relation to . . ."

In any case, *Dasein* comes to light in "no-thing" as pure relation, as pure being-in-the-world, without having a correlate within this world. Every relation to be-ing is rooted in this pure relation as in the necessary condition of its possibility. Care and concern are possible only because of the fundamental fact that man is primordially "relation to . . . ," and it is precisely this most fundamental structure that manifests itself to *Dasein* in dread. In my knowing, my loving, my concernful dealing with intraworldly be-ings, I cannot be "related to" and within these relations understand what I am involved in unless I am absolutely and fundamentally a be-ing whose being itself implies "being related to" and, in this "being related to," primordial "understanding." Since I am thus always connected with being and move about in an understanding of being, the roots of my understanding of being and therefore also of my primordial relation to being must be found in the fundamental dimension of my own being that in dread becomes manifest to me. These roots of being are phenomenologically still hidden in dread and therefore they appear to me phenomenologically as "no-thing." This is the reason why an existential analysis of dread is of fundamental importance.

Heidegger again takes up the problem in *What is Metaphysics?* and here too he starts from the phenomenon of dread. "Although dread is always 'dread of . . . ,' it is not dread of this or that. 'Dread of . . .' is always 'dread about . . .' but not about this or that. The indefinite character of which and about which we are in dread is not just a lack of definiteness, but the essential impossibility of defining 'what' we dread."[22] Here also the term or cause of dread is called "no-thing" because

[22]*Was ist Metaphysik?*, p. 32.

of its indefiniteness. "With the fundamental mood of dread we have reached that event in our *Dasein* in which 'no-thing' reveals itself and which must become the starting point of our inquiry into 'no-thing.' "[23] This term of dread can be phenomenologically indicated only as "no-thing" since it is not a be-ing and, moreover, still remains concealed.

This "no-thing" could be described as pure openness, the fact itself of "being open to. . . ." Even more profoundly, it may be described as that which gives a be-ing the possibility of "being open." "Only in the clear night of dread's 'no-thing' does the primordial openness of be-ing as such arise: that it is a be-ing and not 'no-thing.' "[24] Here Heidegger goes beyond what he has said in *Being and Time,* although his expressions are still chosen in such a way that there remain several possibilities.

Positivity of "No-thing"

It is important to notice that with "no-thing" Heidegger here wants to indicate something positive: "no-thing" makes it possible for us to understand in a primordial wonder that which is both most mysterious and most trivial, namely, that there are be-ings and that there is not nothing. The fact that be-ings can manifest themselves in this way as be-ings and that as such they can be objects of our wonder means that they appear precisely in their being and free themselves from the background of what is unquestioned obviousness.

Accordingly, if we wonder about be-ing as be-ing, if we look at it as such, then it detaches itself from a more primordial and also more familiar horizon which precisely makes this wonder possible, but which is not itself a be-ing since the emergence of any be-ing becomes possible precisely because of it. It is the phenomenal abyss of "no-thing" that manifests itself here as "being" and

[23]*Ibid.,* p. 33
[24]*Ibid.,* p. 34.

that is the norm of every statement about being and the condition of its possibility. " 'No-thing' is that which makes the revelation of be-ing as such possible for man's *Dasein*."[25] Thus what announces itself phenomenally as "no-thing" is that which makes be-ing as such possible and therefore also its becoming unconcealed, its *a-letheia*.[26]

"No-thing" is Being

These expressions still remain vague and ambiguous, so that one can interpret them in very different ways. They can be explained in terms of what Heidegger says in *Being and Time* and in *The Essence of Ground*.

However, a very different explanation is possible if one investigates how Heidegger has developed these thoughts in his later works. Many have seen a new philosophy in these developments. It seems, however, that he remains in the same ontological sphere though his initial vision is now expressed more lucidly and more sharply. More precisely expressed, for many years Heidegger stood at crossroads and only relatively late did he definitively reject one of the two possibilities and interpret his earlier work from the stand he has accepted in his later works.

Anyhow, in 1943 Heidegger taught a course on Parmenides and Heraclitus in which he said: "We must try to reflect on Being itself. . . . This kind of thinking is sudden, it can be attained time and time again only by a leap, a jumping from be-ing into the bottomless abyss. . . . There are no 'explanatory bridges.' All explaining which remains on the 'basis of facts' is like building [a bridge] on marsh ground. It carries weight only because one forgets Being. Being gives no footing but is bottomless. It remains without footing and ground and does not need any. It does not spring from the solid soil of be-ings, as something that can be rooted in this soil. To be solidly rooted belongs only to be-ings in relation to Being. To

---

[25]*Ibid.*, p. 35
[26]*Ibid.*, pp. 40-41.

be without solid roots appears to be a defect only in the case of be-ings, in which *we* lose all support."[27]

Heidegger maintains here that Being itself has no ground, that Being makes be-ings possible as be-ings and that Being is the ground of truth. These assertions agree fully with what he has said earlier about "no-thing." Being manifests itself *to us* in the phenomenon of dread as "no-thing," as that which has no ground since in it we lose all support. These same thoughts are contained in the Postscript of *What is Metaphysics?,* which also dates from 1943: "A renewed study of this lecture may show whether 'no-thing,' which determines the essence of dread, is exhausted by a pure negation of all be-ing, or whether that which never and nowhere is a be-ing unveils itself as that which differs from every be-ing and is called by us 'Being.' "[28] In this text "no-thing" is explicitly said to be Being as Being primordially presents itself to us. Thus the view proposed in *Being and Time* appears to be in harmony with the one given in his later works.

Moreover, the dynamism of the relation between Being and *Dasein* appears now to arise from Being and not from man's understanding. Dread does not constitute "no-thing," but Being constitutes dread. Being makes *Dasein* be understanding of being. According to Heidegger, all this becomes evident when one reflects again on *What is Metaphysics?* and personally tries to see the truth of its assertions in the light of phenomenology.

Heidegger also mentions in the Postscript that we become disloyal to thinking if we glibly equate "no-thing" with pure nothing and call it nonexistent. Instead, we must always remain ready to "experience [in 'no-thing'] the vastness of that which gives every be-ing the 'pass' to be. That is Being itself."[29] It is Being itself that raises

---

[27]Quoted by B. Welte, "Remarques sur l'ontologie de Heidegger," *Revue des sciences philosophiques et théologiques,* vol. 31 (1947), pp. 379-393.
[28]*Was ist Metaphysik?,* p. 45.
[29]*Ibid.,* pp. 45-46.

its voice, that appeals to man, not in his feelings and strivings, but in his own being, his essence. Man is man because he knows that he is called by the voice of Being, by Being that originally in dread became disclosed to him as "no-thing."

4. BEING AND BEING

Finally we must ask what exactly Heidegger means by being and especially by Being. What does he refer to when he maintains that "forgetfulness of Being" and of the distinction between Being and being has dominated the entire history of philosophy since Plato? What is this Being that metaphysics has always forgotten to mention, though it was always implicitly present as a hidden foundation in all its speculations?

In his answer to these questions Heidegger is aware of the fact that it is very difficult to speak about that which lies at the root of all philosophical thought and which even seems to transcend the possibilities of any philosophical approach. What does one call that which lies at the source of every name and every term and how can one grasp in a definition that which precisely escapes from every limiting definition? According to Heidegger, Being itself remains "still unspoken."[30]

To attain Being itself and express it, there has first to be an immediate experience of Being itself. Only on the basis of such an experience can the standpoint of traditional metaphysics be transcended. "But Being—what is it? It is Itself. Future thinking must learn to experience and express it in words."[31] It is possible that our lack of an appropriate "language" still prevents us from saying what Being itself is, but at least we can start to search for and think about Being.[32]

In this search it is, of course, of the utmost importance that the right approach be chosen. The right approach is

---

[30]*Ibid.*, p. 9.
[31]*Brief über den Humanismus*, p. 76.
[32]*Was ist Metaphysik?*, p. 10.

not necessarily the shortest route, for the right way is often found only after making a difficult choice at several crossroads. "Nevertheless, Being can somehow be approached—by meandering dead-end forest trails (*Holzwege*). Such trails are overgrown because they are but rarely used and always end on untrodden ground. One can easily get lost on them. Yet these trails themselves always wander their way in one and the same forest—the forest of one and the same Being."[33] At any rate the right way is never a road ahead but rather a return to the foundations of metaphysics,[34] or more correctly, a "step back from metaphysics into its essence."[35]

What Being is Not

It is not very difficult to indicate what Heidegger certainly does not mean by Being. "Being is not God and not a 'foundation of the world' (*Weltgrund*). Being is farther away than all be-ings and at the same time nearer to man than any be-ing, whether this be-ing be a rock, an animal, a work of art, a machine, an angel, or God. Being is closest of all."[36] Being cannot be identical with any of the finite be-ings which we encounter in the world; it is not even the highest be-ing, the first principle from which everything comes through creation or emanation, and about which traditional philosophy speaks.

This statement, of course, does not yet make any positive assertion with respect to God. The question, "How does God come into philosophy, not only modern philosophy but philosophy as such?"[37] has to be treated elsewhere. Presently Heidegger merely says that Being itself cannot be God, not any particular be-ing, not the sum total of all be-ings, and not be-ing as a whole. Usually man

---

[33]K. Löwith, *Heidegger, Denker in dürftiger Zeit,* Frankfurt a.M., 1953, p. 27.
[34]*Was ist Metaphysik?*, p. 9.
[35]*Identität und Differenz,* p. 47.
[36]*Brief über den Humanismus,* p. 76.
[37]*Identität und Differenz,* p. 52.

limits his considerations to be-ings and does not expressly
ask about Being itself; on the other hand, in all his considerations of be-ings man is in relation with Being itself,
be it unconsciously.[38] "No matter how be-ing be explained,
whether as spirit in the sense of spiritualism or as matter
and energy in the sense of materialism, whether as becoming and life or as 'representation,' as will, substance,
subject, *energeia* or as the eternal return of the same,
every time be-ing appears in the light of Being."[39]

As we have already seen, for man Being itself always
assumes at first the form of a "no-thing," the "no-thing of
be-ings." Starting from be-ings, man always experiences
Being as "no-thing."[40] "This the purely 'other' than all
be-ings is 'Non-be-ing.' But this 'no-thing' 'comes to be
present' (*west*) as Being."[41]

Positive Description of Being

If one tries to express Being in a more positive sense,
it should be described as that which lets be-ings and
Dasein be, makes them be, and gives them their ground.
In the most primordial sense this "making be" and ground-
ing is not a producing, a creating or a causing. These
further determinations of "making be" are not necessarily
meaningless, but fail to express its most primordial and
radical meaning. Being itself is that which lets things be
primordially *as* be-ings, it originally uncovers them, it
makes them come to light and stand in unconcealment
(*a-letheia*). The primordial experience of Being itself in
this sense is essentially connected with the essence of truth
considered as *a-letheia*.

In this way it can be explained that Heidegger's thinking, which since *Being and Time* has always presented
itself as a return to the foundations and an inquiry into
the meaning of being, can actually present itself as a con-

[38]*Brief über den Humanismus*, p. 76.
[39]*Was ist Metaphysik?*, p. 7.
[40]*Ibid.*, pp. 37, 41; *Vom Wesen des Grundes*, p. 5.
[41]*Was ist Metaphysik?*, p. 45.

stantly more penetrating reflection upon the essence and origin of truth. The word "truth" shows us the way to answer the question about the essential meaning of being. "*A-letheia* could be the word which gives us a hitherto unexperienced 'wink' in the unthought 'essence' of Being (*esse*)."[42]

What exactly should be understood here by "essence" and "truth"? "Essence" here does not mean *essentia* as "quiddity" nor does it refer to the first component of the classical pair *essentia* and *existentia*. For Heidegger the expression "going back to the essence of something" means to let something appear in its being, in its primordial way of emerging. This "going back" requires that one shows what is really at work in the heart of this "emerging." Essence is certainly synonymous with "that which a being is," but the emphasis should be put on the "*is*." The German *Wesen,* translated here as "essence," is connected with the old verb *wesen,* which means "to be" in a sense that is somehow active.[43]

5. THE ESSENCE OF TRUTH

The Essence of Truth in "Being and Time"

Heidegger first speaks about the essence of truth in *Being and Time* when he discusses the connection between *logos* and *phaenomenon.* He calls a phenomenon "that which shows itself in itself, the manifest."[44] To be able to show itself the phenomenon must already stand in the clarity of something that is a light. The phenomenon can be approached only because the *logos*[45] lets it be seen. This *logos* can uncover or conceal things; it can let things be true or false. *Logos,* then, brings things to light in a true or in an untrue way. Since the being of be-ings is

[42]*Ibid.,* p. 11.
[43]*Einführung in die Metaphysik,* p. 55.
[44]*S.Z.,* p. 28.
[45]*Logos* has the same root as the verb *legein,* to speak.

what is most concealed in them, it needs to be explicitly brought to light in a phenomenological way.

In *Being and Time* the *logos* that brings to light is *Dasein*. "What is primarily 'true,' that is, uncovering, is *Dasein*."[46] As being simultaneously thrown into existence and projecting itself from there, *Dasein* is both uncovering and concealing, both in the truth and in untruth.[47] For this reason "all truth is relative to *Dasein's* being because the kind of being that is essential to truth is characterized by *Dasein*."[48] "There is" (*es gibt*) truth only so long as there is a *Dasein*. The laws of Newton, the principle of non-contradiction, and any other truth are true only so long as there is a *Dasein*. Before there was a *Dasein* and after all *Daseins* will have ceased to be, there was no truth and there will be no truth, since truth can then not be as unconcealedness, as uncovering and as being uncovered.[49]

In other words, man does not accept truth because there are eternal truths, but only because he himself is already presupposed as a finite *Dasein* that is thrown into openness and projects other be-ings in its being, that discloses and uncovers them: man is already *de facto* there and always *de facto* has to be there. But why should *Dasein* always be, and therefore why should be-ings always be uncovered; why should there always be truth? So long as one cannot explain this point, any assertion of "eternal" truth remains a "fanciful claim."[50] According to Heidegger, this is all one can say about these problems within the context of a preliminary analysis of *Dasein* in which one limits oneself to a description of what presents itself immediately. So long as the question of the meaning of being remains unsolved, Heidegger hold that nothing more is to be said about truth.

[46] *S.Z.*, p. 220.
[47] *S.Z.*, p. 223.
[48] *S.Z.*, p. 227.
[49] *S.Z.*, pp. 226-227.
[50] *S.Z.*, p. 227.

The Essence of Truth in Heidegger's Later Works

Heidegger's ideas developed further in his work *The Essence of Truth* and subsequent publications. At least from 1947 on, they took an entirely different direction than had originally been expected. Lines of thinking which at first seemed to point in one direction, on closer inspection and in a more profound perspective, revealed themselves to deviate considerably from the expected course. Although Heidegger in his later work maintains in essence what he has said in *Being and Time,* the *ultimate* foundation of truth is no longer seen to lie in *Dasein* but in Being. Man is only the "locus" of the truth of Being. Our projects do not decide truth and untruth, but the only thing of importance is whether Being itself from its own truth is able to bring about a relation to the essence of man by virtue of which man is brought within the domain of being itself.

At first Heidegger did not delve into the question on what this "being able" ultimately depends. It seemed as if Being itself and even God owe it to man that there is a dwelling place for them in which they can be present; they cannot be present if man would not, so to speak, meet them halfway. Later in his life, however, Heidegger arrives at the opposite view. In his *Letter on Humanism* he writes: "Man is . . . 'thrown' into the truth of being by Being itself, 'ex-sisting' in this way, the shepherd of the truth of Being in order that be-ings appear as the be-ings they are in the light of Being. Man does not decide whether and how God and gods, history and nature come into the clarity of Being, are present there or absent. A be-ing's coming into this clarity depends upon the 'mission' (*Geschick*) of Being."[51]

It is important to note that at the same time *Dasein* itself also obtains a more profound meaning, for the emphasis in the explanation of *Dasein's* own being is increasingly

---

[51]*Brief über den Humanismus,* p. 75.

shifted from project to care.[52] The *ex* of "existence" no longer indicates merely being open to and going out to the world, but refers now primarily to the possibility of listening to Being, of letting oneself be called by Being and to be faithful to this call.[53] The same applies to the *"Da"* of *Dasein.* It no longer means only that man is a being-in-the-world which can project a world in which be-ings can appear as be-ings, but it means now that the world is a dwelling place of man only because man dwells in the truth of Being. "Man is present in such a way that he is the *'Da,'* the 'clearing,' of Being. This 'being' of *'Da'* and only this is fundamentally characterized by ex-sistence, that is, by standing 'ec-statically' in the truth of Being. The 'ec-static' essence of man lies in ex-sistence, which remains different from the *existentia* spoken of by metaphysics."[54]

Truth and Being

Finally it is also important to note that, according to Heidegger's latest works, man can approach the truth of Being only through an immediate "experience" of Being itself.[55] The experiences of traditional metaphysics, which speak only of be-ing as be-ing, cannot possibly be identified with the experience in question, for Being wholly escapes every form of representative thinking. Even phenomenological experience, as it is provisionally described in *Being and Time,* does not appear to have any meaning here, since this experience too refers to im-mediately given be-ings. The experience in question refers only to Being itself and even emanates from it. "Experi-ence is a mode of being present (*Anwesen*), that is, of Being."[56] Man has part in this presence of Being; keep-

---

[52]*Ibid.*, p. 76.

[53]*Was ist das—die Philosophie?*, pp. 46-48.

[54]*Brief über den Humanismus*, p. 69.

[55]*Ibid.*, p. 76; *Was ist Metaphysik?*, p. 9.

[56]*Was ist Metaphysik?*, pp. 7-9; *Holzwege,* pp. 168-170.

ing himself "near to Being"[57] is for man the necessary condition on which any be-ing whatsoever can appear to him. Finally, to this presence of Being itself to man there corresponds a movement on the side of man, which one could call with Hegel "dialectical."[58]

All this, however, does not help very much to clarify what Being itself is. Thinkers of the future will have to discover this.[59] In the meantime Being remains something "unsaid."[60] Provisionally we will have to be satisfied with "thinking about it" on the basis of the existing metaphysics though we know that Being itself does not belong to the domain of metaphysics. But we know already that the road to any knowledge of Being must consist in reflection on the origin and essence of truth.

6. METAPHYSICS, BEING AND GOD

"Onto-Theo-Logic"

In *Identity and Difference* Heidegger sees the fundamental mistake of traditional metaphysics in the fact that since Plato philosophers have forgotten or neglected the essential difference between being and Being. For this reason their thinking degenerated into an "onto-theo-logy," which reached its peak with Hegel. If, however, one dares to think about this difference explicitly and thematically, then it becomes immediately evident that the traditional concepts of being and of God are not acceptable. The being of traditional metaphysics and the God of which it speaks are not the true Being and the true God, but they are only forms of our representative thinking.

For this reason it would be desirable no longer to speak of God within traditional metaphysics. "Metaphysics is 'onto-theo-logy.' Anyone who has, through his own development, experienced theology, whether that of the

---

[57]*Brief über den Humanismus*, p. 85.
[58]*Ibid.*, p. 94; *Holzwege*, pp. 168-169.
[59]*Brief über den Humanismus*, p. 76.
[60]*Was ist Metaphysik?*, p. 9.

Christian faith or that of philosophy, nowadays prefers to be silent about God so far as thinking is concerned. For the onto-theo-logical character of metaphysics has become questionable to thinking people, not because of some kind of atheism, but because of an experience of thinking in which the still *unthought* unity of the essence of metaphysics revealed itself in onto-theo-logy."[61]

Western metaphysics has spoken much about God without being able to reach Him to whom this name referred. He shows Himself only to a thinking that knows how to unmask metaphysics' forgetfulness and dares to think about the relevant problems in terms of the difference between being and Being precisely insofar as they are different. Despite all its talk about God, traditional metaphysics is, seen from this new standpoint, atheistic. For it conceives God as a be-ing, be it the supreme be-ing; yet a be-ing discovered on the basis of be-ings can never really be God. From the standpoint of a more profound philosophy and from that of Christian theology, one must object to Hegel's idea of God as well as to the whole of traditional metaphysics.

The God of metaphysics "is the Cause as *Causa sui* and this is the appropriate name for God in philosophy. To this God man cannot pray or bring a sacrifice. Before the *Causa sui* man cannot fall on his knees in awe, nor can he play music or dance for Him. In this sense godless thinking, which must give up the God of philosophy, God as *Causa sui,* is perhaps closer to the 'godly' God. In this context that means that god-less thinking is freer for Him than onto-theo-logic would be willing to admit."[62] This insight into the ungodliness of the God of traditional metaphysics is only possible to a thinking that dares to "take the 'step back,' . . . back from the forgetfulness of the difference as such into the 'mission' (*Geschick*) of the concealment of the issue which escapes us."[63]

[61]*Identität und Differenz,* p. 51.
[62]*Ibid.,* pp. 70-71.
[63]*Ibid.,* p. 71

Thinking About the "Godly" God

What can this thinking teach us about God? As he had done in his earlier works with respect to Being, Heidegger remarks that it is very difficult to say something about God since traditional metaphysics, from Plato to Hegel, has deformed all philosophical terms in function of its onto-theo-logic. All philosophical terms which have been standardized by metaphysics become insufficient and misleading as soon as one penetrates into the dimension of Being itself. How could one still speak here about substance, unity, act, subject, foundation, ground, principle, spirit, or God, since all these terms have already been appropriated by a philosophy that has forgotten Being itself but continues to speak about the being of be-ings?

Lack of words makes a thinker now practically helpless before Being. One must even admit that it remains open to question "whether the Western languages have been stamped exclusively with the seal of metaphysics and therefore ultimately with that of onto-theo-logic or whether these languages offer other possibilities of speaking as well as of 'saying nothing while speaking.' "[64]

It is evident, in any case, that the new thinking that is supposed to replace traditional metaphysics will have to be a genuine thinking about Being and that, instead of the accepted usual theology, there will have to be a genuine thinking about the "godly God." An effort must be made to think of Being itself in such a way that it no longer resembles a be-ing, a category, an essence, or anything else pertaining to the realm of representative thinking. It is also certain that in Being itself there can be no question of a distinction between subject and object, for Being transcends all distinctions, those between subject and object as well as those between I and world, between theoretical and practical reason, between physical

---

[64]*Ibid.*, p. 72.

and ethical ideas.[65]   Being itself therefore cannot be defined in logical terms, but simply "is it itself."[66]   It can be experienced in its fullness only in the lightening existence that man himself is.

The Road to Being

The road to Being can only be cleared in what Heidegger calls primordial *Er-eignis*. He derives this term, which ordinarily means "event," from *er-äugen,* to discern with the eyes and thus to appropriate. *"Er-eignis 'ap-prop-riates' (vereignet)* man and Being in their essential togetherness."[67] It is "the internally vibrating realm through which man and Being reach each other in their 'essence' and become what they are by losing the determinations which metaphysics has imputed to them."[68]   Through a leap from traditional metaphysics, which ultimately rests upon the principle of identity, and even from every intentional form of foundation, man's thinking must try to reach the identity of Being as in an abyss. "But this groundless abyss *(Abgrund)* is neither pure nothing nor a dark confusion, but *Er-eignis.*"[69] This leap into the identity which is Being itself is necessary if the principle of identity is to play its fundamental role in man's intentional thinking about be-ings.

In this way Heidegger refers to this mysterious *Er-eignis* to formulate the extremely difficult problem regarding the relation between thinking that is identical with being and thinking that gives be-ings their foundation. Only thinking that is identical with being is able to give the necessary room to thinking that gives be-ings their foundation.[70] Traditional metaphysics, which tries to assign a foundation to be-ings, is correctly understood only

---

[65]*Brief über den Humanismus,* pp. 98-104.
[66]*Ibid.,* p. 76.
[67]*Identität und Differenz,* p. 31.
[68]*Ibid.,* p. 30.
[69]*Ibid.,* p. 32.
[70]*Ibid.,* p. 44.

if it is viewed in the perspective of the true Being. True Being is identity, it differs in principle from the being of be-ings as such and should be called the "pre-intentional," the primordial *Er-eignis.*

Likewise, only in the perspective of Being itself as *Er-eignis* does it become possible to let the true God, the Holy One, appear. He cannot be called here the first, the supreme be-ing, the Cause of himself and of everything else, for here we have precisely left the domain of be-ings through our leap into Being itself. "Only in the perspective of the truth of Being can the 'essence' of the Holy be thought of. Only in terms of the 'essence' of the Holy can the 'essence' of God be thought of. Only in the light of the 'essence' of the Divinity can one think and say what the term 'God' is supposed to name."[71]

Accordingly, Heidegger speaks about Being itself in a hesitant way and is even more reserved in speaking about God. He thinks that the time has not yet come to develop his idea of God. Our era is still too much permeated with traditional metaphysics. This metaphysics has imprinted its mark on our language to such an extent that provisionally our first task lies in attuning man to the question of the meaning of Being and to everything implied in this question. Man must first be called back to the interiority of Being itself, or rather to the *Er-eignis* "in which man and Being are 'ap-propriated' (*ge-eignet*) to each other."[72] In any case, God is not one who can be demonstrated. Likewise, He neither reveals Himself in an immediate intuition nor can be presupposed as a postulate. God is the one who eternally conceals Himself. His appearance is a mystery to man, but this mystery cannot be avoided by anyone who seriously thinks about Being.

---

[71]*Brief über den Humanismus,* p. 102.
[72]*Identität und Differenz,* p. 28.

CHAPTER TWELVE

EPILOGUE

In concluding this modest introduction to the thought and work of Martin Heidegger, we would like to add a few words of appraisal. To present in a condensed form a substantial judgment on the philosophy of a great thinker is not easy. On the other hand, it would make little sense to limit ourselves to the assertion that Heidegger undoubtedly is one of the greatest thinkers of our time, and that many of the ideas which he has propounded since the publication of *Being and Time* appear to be of lasting value for philosophy. True as such a statement may be, it becomes acceptable only when it is explained and justified. Such an approach, however, is beyond the scope of this little book.

There is also another reason why such a declaration of value would be of little merit. Experience shows that an assertion of this kind is often completely misunderstood by readers who are not very familiar with philosophy—particularly contemporary philosophy—or prefer a different trend of philosophy. All too often the latter view such an approval as an implicit disapproval of all other ways of thinking and in particular of all philosophical movements of the past.

Such an interpretation, however, is patently wrong, especially with regard to Heidegger's philosophy. First of all, from beginning to end, his thinking proceeds in a living dialogue with all the important trends of philosophical thinking from antiquity to the present. Heidegger's work is not even comprehensible unless it is viewed in the context of this dialogue with past and present thinkers. On the other hand, this same dialogue with the main streams of philosophy is a major obstacle when one tries to penetrate to the core of Heidegger's train of thoughts.

Secondly, Heidegger considers philosophy a very personal matter and in no way a question of merely adopting views in a passive way. Man's being is, according to him, essentially temporal and historical. Consequently, man's personal philosophy implies essentially a dialogue with the past and *a fortiori* with contemporary thinking. Therefore, there is no room here for contrasts and much less for opposing "antiquated" to "modern," as young people especially are prone to do in their impatience with the "past." Anyone who represents matters in that way shows that he has not yet understood much of what has happened in philosophy since Hegel. Finally, such a standpoint conflicts not only with the essentially historical character of philosophical thinking, but also with the relativity that is essentially implied in any human perspective and in some way also in every philosophical viewpoint.

In the following pages we will try to develop these points to some extent.

The Personal Character of Philosophy

The first point of which we should be profoundly convinced is that philosophy is not a matter of harmonious syntheses, formulated once and for all by a few superior minds, which subsequently are to be accepted by everyone else in a "passive" way. To begin with, there are not yet any perfect philosophical syntheses and there will not ever be any, because the perfect synthesis essentially transcends man's powers. Secondly, since there exist many syntheses, it is ultimately through our personal insight that we have to decide which of these syntheses we find most acceptable. Philosophy is a strictly personal affair. "Philosophical thinking must at all times be original. Every man must do it for himself."[1]

---

[1] Karl Jaspers, *Einführung in die Philosophie,* München, 1957, p. 9.

Martin Heidegger

The Historical Character of Philosophy

The idea, however, that philosophy is essentially personal must not be understood in a one-sided way, but should be complemented by the historical character of all personal thinking. Although every philosopher must strive for a personal form of thinking, it is nonetheless an illusion to hold that this personal thinking can be done independently of the philosophical tradition. Man's way of living in the world is essentially a taking up of history, for his existence is not only openness to a world but also openness to the future on the basis of a definite and given past.[2] This past on which and from which we live, is not limited to our own individual history, but also encompasses the past of all those with whom we communicate. In the last analysis it extends to the past of all mankind.

Every human activity bears the mark of being-conditioned by a historical situation. This statement applies also to our most personal philosophizing. It too is always a thinking within the boundaries of a particular philosophical tradition because our own thinking is to some extent dependent on philosophical tradition in its problematics and its method. In our philosophical thinking we are always heirs of a certain past, even when we are not aware of it or dislike it. This relationship between our philosophizing and the philosophical life of the past has two aspects. On the one hand, the philosophical tradition is of necessity a source with respect to our own contemporary thinking; but on the other, this necessity always contains the grave risk that our own thinking will never reach the level of true and authentic philosophizing.

Thus our philosophical thinking always and of necessity has its starting point in an existing situation which is explicitly or implicitly determined by the history of philosophy. All systematic thinking in philosophy is essentially a historical thinking, every systematic philosophical

[2]William A. Luijpen, *Existential Phenomenology,* Pittsburgh, 4th impr., 1965, pp. 4-9.

problem implies or perhaps even *is* a historical problem. The philosophical past is never a complete loss for us because it helps us to penetrate into the present and it enriches our presence in being. The elements of genuine greatness contained in the thinking of a great philosopher are not buried in the darkness of a past that is gone forever, although it is true that without our own thinking they will never again come to life. The fact, however, that the thinking of past philosophers comes to life in us, makes us transcend the narrow limitations of our finite minds. Without the great thinkers of the past, we would be less attuned to the mystery of being which permeates and supports us.

The Necessity of Making a Choice

It is impossible, however, to master the history of philosophy in its entirety. First of all, a single person cannot read, study, and experience everything that hundreds of great philosophers have presented. Secondly, in our reading we understand only those things of the past which in some way appeal to us as being congenial to our own thinking.[3] As Hegel says, "The living spirit which dwells in a philosophy, requires to be reborn by a kindred spirit in order to reveal itself."

Consequently our taking up of the philosophical past will always and of necessity have a limited nature, i.e., it will imply a choice. Here we meet a first possible danger. Although the finiteness of our mind to some extent necessitates this choice, the more one-sided this choice is and the more its limitation is arbitrary, the more dangerous it is. There is another and even greater danger in this contact with a particular philosophical tradition. This second danger is so great that in many cases it has given the death blow to authentic and personal thinking. Our living and thinking is essentially a taking up of history; yet,

---

[3]Maurice Merleau-Ponty, *Phénoménologie de la Perception,* Paris, 1945, p. ii.

despite the fact that our own grasp of being is orientated and nourished by that of the past, our entrance into history demands also that we remain ourselves.

To retain our self-identity as thinkers, we must first look at this past as from a distance in order to let it appear to us as it really was. Only then can we ask how this past thinking can be reactivated, how it can be taken up again by determining our standpoint toward it.

Dialectical Relation with the Past

Accordingly, when we say that our philosophical thinking takes up a philosophical tradition, we intend to express that our contemporary thinking is essentially historical, that it inevitably has its roots in the past. All genuinely human thinking is necessarily a thinking on the basis of a historical situation. Any thinking which denies this fact is not genuinely human thinking, or else it is thinking which fails to understand itself. The sense of this assertion, however, should not be misunderstood.

First of all, it is not a matter of becoming first involved in contemporary thinking and only then asking, *post factum,* how this thinking should be situated and based on any particular philosophical tradition. Secondly, it is also incorrect to ask how the thinking of the past which I take up must be adjusted to contemporary thinking. It seems to us that in both cases one isolates two aspects which essentially go together. Between our contemporary thinking and the philosophical thinking of the past there exists essentially a dialectical relationship. If one aspect is divorced from the other, there remains only an *abstractum.* All genuinely philosophical thinking is necessarily contemporary thinking, but as such it is also essentially the taking up of a certain tradition. It is hardly necessary to add that few philosophers are explicitly aware of these genetic relations.

It is important to realize that this taking up of the past cannot consist either in "passively" rethinking certain philosophical insights or in extending and completing what the great thinkers of the past have left unfinished. Taking up a philosophical tradition means largely to assume again a genuinely philosophical attitude and to rethink the age-old problems in a personal way. This personal rethinking is not a question of rewording what has already been said. It is not even, at least not primarily, a question of trying to find new solutions for these problems. Our primary task is to reconsider those same age-old problems in the light of a fundamental "primitive fact," a "central reference point."[4] This leads us to a final point which seems of special importance in this context.

Fundamental Intuition

Every philosopher starts from his own specific fundamental intuition, his own "primitive fact," his own "central point of reference." In every philosophy there is an all-illuminating light which enables the philosopher to bring clarity in the complexity of the reality he wants to explain. It would not be difficult to illustrate this in the philosophies of Plato, Aristotle, the Scholastics, Descartes, Spinoza, Kant, Hegel, Bergson and many others.

There is no philosophy which stops in front of the multiplicity and the complexity of what is immediately given in experience and which is satisfied with a random summing up of "everything that is." Philosophy is not "a tale told by an idiot," but an attempt to reduce the multitude of data to a comprehensible unity by laying bare its structures and arranging them in an orderly fashion. In this attempt the philosopher does not *a priori* know

---

[4]Cf. Merleau-Ponty, *Sens et Non-sens, Paris,* 1948, pp. 165-198; A. De Waelhens, *Une philosophie de l'ambiguïté. L'existentialisme de Maurice Merleau-Ponty,* Louvain, 1951, pp. 331-365; A. Dondeyne, *Contemporary European Thought and Christian Faith,* Pittsburgh, 2nd impr., 1963, pp. 36-66; Dondeyne, "L'historicité dans la philosophie contemporaine," *Revue philosophique de Louvain,* vol. LIV (1956), pp. 5-25, pp. 456-477; E. Fink, *Zur ontologischen Frühgeschichte von Raum—Zeit—Bewegung,* The Hague, 1957, pp. 14-21.

what kind of unity there will be and how its structures and its order will be laid bare. The light of the fundamental intuition is not itself first uncovered and then "put to work." Every new philosophy starts from a fundamental but vague idea that a certain approach will perhaps lead to results, long before the philosopher is able to explain what exactly he is doing, by what principles he is guided, and by which light he will ultimately try to bring clarity to "everything that is."

It stands to reason that every philosophy will be successful precisely to the extent to which the chosen approach really offers a possibility to understand the multiplicity and the complexity of the given reality by disclosing its harmonious unity.[5]

It is difficult to say how such a starting point precisely is chosen, for this choice is not always made in the same manner. It can be stated, however, that such a fundamental intuition is prescribed, as it were, by the era in which the philosopher lived and especially by the dialectical relationship with the past which he managed to establish in his time. Such an approach is often chosen because other approaches have already turned out to be leading nowhere or at least did not offer any longer the possibility to throw a clear light on the fundamental problems of philosophy within the context of the era's intellectual preoccupations. Sometimes also an intuition from the past is taken up again in a more radical way. Occasionally there is a kind of oscillating movement between extremes which in a vague dialectical process leads toward a new synthesis.

What matters to us here is that the starting point of a philosophy lies in a personal and often ingenious intuition, which, however, is based on, or rather motivated by, the dialectical relationship between one's own era and traditional thought.

---

[5]Dondeyne, *Contemporary European Thought and Christian Faith,* pp. 54-58; Luijpen, *op. cit.,* pp. 34-35.

Heidegger's Dialogue with the Past

To return to Heidegger's philosophy, it is easy to see that his philosophy is important for us, first of all, because it shows in an eminent way how much contemporary thinking must be rooted in the thinking of the past and how traditional thinking can again come to live in today's thinking by way of a dialectical tension. It suffices here to refer to Heidegger's reflections on the ideas of Parmenides, Aristotle, Descartes, Kant, Hegel, Kierkegaard, Nietzsche, Husserl and so many others. No matter how incidental these reflections at times may be, they always illustrate a genuine contact.

A second important point seems the following. Considering the historical tradition of Aristotle and scholasticism, Descartes, Hegel and the various "irrationalistic" and "positivistic" movements of the nineteenth century, Heidegger's philosophy begins exactly where, from a philosophical viewpoint, modern man should really begin —namely, with the fact that man is essentially being-in-the-world. From such a starting point the genuine wealth of Greek and medieval philosophy can come to a harmonious synthesis with the genuine plenitude of modern thinking since Descartes. Such a synthesis could become a guiding light to the chaos of contemporary man on his uncertain journey, insofar as it makes man understand himself in terms of his *real* nature and insofar as it ultimately forces him to transcend his being-in-the-world toward the Absolute, no matter how laborious such a transcending may be.

Relativity

All this does not mean, however, that Heidegger's philosophy is a definitive form of philosophy, for his thinking, too, is and remains thinking from an historical perspective. Heidegger speaks of "keeping everything in suspense," to emphasize that in his living contact with other forms of perspectivistic thinking he is clearly aware of the finiteness and relativity of his own thinking. On the other hand, his thinking fundamentally goes beyond this finiteness and this relativity, without ever being able to overcome them completely.

To accept such a relativity does not in the least appear dangerous to us, provided we keep in mind that every form of genuine philosophizing is an authentic attempt to throw light on the truth about man, be-ings, and the world, about the being of be-ings and about Being itself.

Precisely this intentional relationship between our philosophical thinking and "everything that is" prevents the relativity of every philosophical vision from becoming completely meaningless, for this intentionality provides it with a direction, a meaning. On the other hand, we think that this conception of historicity and relativity can find its definitive foundation only in a philosophical explanation of our transcendence as "being toward the Absolute." According to Heidegger, the time for such an explanation has not yet arrived because the difference between be-ing and Being has first to be placed in a sharper focus.

BIBLIOGRAPHY

Heidegger's Main Works

Die Lehre vom Urteil im Psychologismus. Ein kritisch-positiver Beitrag zur Logik, Leipzig, 1914.

Die Kategorien- und Bedeutungslehre des Duns Scotus, Tübingen, 1916.

Sein und Zeit, first published in 1927. We use the 1953 Tübingen ed.; English translation, *Being and Time,* New York, 1962.

Kant und das Problem der Metaphysik, first published 1929; Frankfurt a.M., 1951. English ed., *Kant and the Problem of Metaphysics,* Bloomington, Ind., 1962.

Vom Wesen des Grundes, first published 1929; Frankfurt a.M., 1955.

Was ist Metaphysik?, first published 1929; Frankfurt a.M., 1955; English ed., *What is Metaphysics?,* in *Existence and Being* by Martin Heidegger, London, n.d.

Die Selbstbehauptung der deutschen Universität, Breslau, 1933.

Hölderlin und das Wesen der Dichtung, München, 1937; English ed., *Hölderlin and the Essence of Poetry,* in *Existence and Being.*

Vom Wesen der Wahrheit, first published 1943; Frankfurt a.M., 1953; English ed., *On the Essence of Truth,* in *Existence and Being.*

Platons Lehre von der Wahrheit. Mit einem Brief über den "Humanismus," Bern, 1947.

Holzwege, first published 1950; Frankfurt a.M., 1957.

Einführung in die Metaphysik, Tübingen, 1953; English ed., *Introduction to Metaphysics,* New Haven, 1959.

Was heisst Denken?, Tübingen, 1954.

Vorträge und Aufsätze, Pfullingen, 1954.

Was ist das—die Philosophie?, Pfullingen, 1956; English ed., *What is Philosophy?,* New York, 1958.

Der Satz vom Grund, Pfullingen, 1957.

Identität und Differenz, Pfullingen, 1957; English ed., *Essays in Metaphysics,* New York, 1962.

Unterwegs zur Sprache, Pfullingen, 1958.

Gelassenheit, Pfullingen, 1959.

Zur Seinsfrage, Frankfurt a.M., 1959; English ed., *The Question of Being,* New York, 1958.

179

Martin Heidegger

SECONDARY REFERENCES

Only those books and articles are listed here which
have been consulted in the preparation of this Introduction.
Its interpretation of Heidegger's *Being and Time* has
been largely guided by the works of de Waelhens, Biemel,
Landgrebe and Löwith. Hühnerfeld supplies a few inter-
esting details about Heidegger's life, but otherwise his
work does not seem to be of much importance. The considerations of Heidegger's language, which do not extend
to his philosophy of language itself, owe much to Aler.
The last chapters show the influence of de Waelhens and
Biemel and, in addition, that of certain works written by
Dondeyne, Birault, Delfgaauw and Welte.

J. Aler, "De taal bij Heidegger," *Alg. Ned. Tijdschrift v.
Wijsbegeerte en Psychologie,* vol. 53 (1961), pp. 241-
260.

B. Allemann, *Hölderlin und Heidegger,* Zürich, 1954.

T. Barth, "Indentität und Differenz. Eine Begegnung
mit M. Heidegger " *Wissenschaft und Weisheit,* vol. 22
(1959), pp. 81-92.

F. Beerling, *Antithesen,* Haarlem, 1935.

W. Biemel, "Heideggers Begriff des Daseins," *Studia
Catholica,* vol. 24 (1949), pp. 113-129.

 Le concept du monde chez Heidegger, Louvain, 1950.

H. Birault, "L'onto-théo-logique hégélienne et la dialec-
tique," *Tijdschrift v. Philosophie,* vol. 20 (1958), pp.
646-723.

 "Existence et vérité d'après Heidegger," *Revue de
métaphysique et de morale,* vol. 65 (1959), pp. 35-87.

F. Bollnow, *Existenzphilosophie,* Stuutgart, 1955.

B. Delfgaauw, "De religieuze vraag als kernpunt van het
denken van Martin Heidegger," *Tijdschrift v. Philosophie,* vol. 16 (1954), pp. 85-102.

 "Heidegger en Sartre," *ibid.,* vol. 10 (1948), pp. 289-
336 and 403-446.

 Wat is Existentialisme?, Amsterdam, 1950.

A. Delp, *Tragische Existenz. Zur Philosophie M. Heidegger,* Freiburg i.Br., 1935.

F. de Rademaker, "Identität und Differenz," *Bijdragen,*
vol. 20 (1959), pp. 157-173.

A. de Waelhens, *Chemins et impasses de l'ontologie hei-
deggerienne. A propos de "Holzwege,"* Louvain, 1953.

 Existence et signification, Louvain, 1958.

 "Heidegger et le problème de la métaphysique,"

Revue philosophique de Louvain, vol. 52 (1954), pp. 110-119.

"Heidegger, Platon et l'humanisme," *ibid.,* vol. 46 (1948), pp. 490-496.

La philosophie de Martin Heidegger, Louvain, 1955.

Phénoménologie et vérité. Essai sur l'évolution de l'idée de vérité chez Husserl et Heidegger, Paris, 1953.

A. Dondeyne, "Beschouwingen bij het atheistisch existentialisme," *Tijdschrift v. Philosophie,* vol. 13 (1951), pp. 3-41.

"La différence ontologique chez M. Heidegger," *Revue philosophique de Louvain,* vol. 56 (1958), pp. 35-62 and 251-293.

"Philosophie van de tijd en metaphysica," *Tijdschrift v. Philosophie,* vol. 21 (1959), pp. 491-517.

P. Furstenau, *Heidegger. Das Gefüge seines Denkens,* Frankfurt a.M., 1958.

H. Gadamar, *Wahrheit und Methode,* Tübingen, 1960.

C. Hoberg, *Das Dasein im Menschen. Die Grundfrage der Heideggerschen Philosophie,* Zeulenroda, 1937.

P. Hünnerfeld, *In Sachen Heidegger. Versuch über ein deutsches Genie,* Hamburg, 1959.

K. Kanthack, *Das Denken Martin Heideggers,* Berlin, 1959.

G. Klenk, "Das doppelte Gesicht Heideggers im Spiegel der jüngsten Kritik," *Gregorianum,* vol. 32 (1951), pp. 290-306.

"Heidegger und Kant," *ibid.,* vol. 34 (1953), pp. 56-71.

L. Landgrebe, *Phänomenologie und Metaphysik,* Hamburg, 1949.

Philosophie der Gegenwart, Bonn, 1952.

T. Langan, *The Meaning of Heidegger,* London, 1959.

J. Lotz, "Denken und Sein nach den jüngsten Veröffentlichungen von M. Heidegger," *Scholastik,* vol. 33 (1958), pp. 81-97.

K. Löwith, *Heidegger, Denker in dürftiger Zeit,* Frankfurt a.M., 1953.

M. Müller, *Existenzphilosophie im geistigen Leben der Gegenwart,* Heidelberg, 1949.

H. Ott, *Denken und Sein. Der Weg Martin Heideggers und der Weg der Theologie,* Zollikon, 1959.

J. Pfeiffer, *Existenzphilosophie,* Leipzig, 1934.

O. Pöggeler, "Jean Wahls Heidegger Deutung," *Zeitschrift f. philos. Forschung,* vol. 12 (1958), pp. 437-458.

W. J. Richardson, *Heidegger. Through Phenomenology to Thought,* The Hague, 1963.

L. Schuwer, "De zijnsleer van M. Heidegger," *Studia Catholica,* vol. 26 (1951), pp. 78-89.

H. Spiegelberg, *The Phenomenological Movement,* The Hague, 1960, 2 vols.

L. Stallaert, *Waarheid en vrijheid,* Rotterdam, 1959.

S. Strasser, "The Concept of Dread in the Philosophy of Heidegger," *The Modern Schoolman,* vol. 35 (1957-58), pp. 1-20.

J. van der Meulen, *Heidegger und Hegel,* Meisenheim a.Gl., 1953.

J. van Slooten, *Inleiding tot het denken van Heidegger,* Assen, 1955.

D. von Uslar, "Vom Wesen der Begegnung im Hinblick auf die Unterscheidung von Selbstsein und Sein bei Heidegger," *Zeitschrift f. philos. Forschung,* vol. 13 (1959), pp. 85-101.

D. Vietta, *Die Seinsfrage bei M. Heidegger,* Stuttgart, 1950.

J. Wahl, "Sur les écrits récents de Heidegger," *Revue de métaphysique et de morale,* vol. 63 (1958), pp. 474-482. *Vers la fin de l'ontologie,* Paris, 1956.

B. Welte, "Remarques sur l'ontologie de Heidegger," *Revue des sciences philosophique et théologique,* vol. 31 (1947), pp. 379-393.

Martin Heidegger zum 70. Geburtstag, Pfullingen, 1959.

For a fairly complete bibliography see H. Lübbe, *Bibliographie der Heidegger-Literatur 1917-1955,* Meisenheim a.Gl., 1957 (also in *Zeitschrift f. philos. Forschung,* vol. 11 (1957), pp. 401-452) and G. Schneeberger, *Erganzungen zu einer Heidegger-Bibliographie,* Bern, 1960.